QUEEI

HERBER₁ ₁AUL

TABLE OF CONTENTS

CHAPTER I: POLITICS — I

It was decreed by Providence that the younger daughter of James Stuart and Anne Hyde should sit upon the throne of England, and be its nominal ruler during a period unsurpassed, throughout English history, for splendour in letters and fame in war. Yet few of her subjects were less fitted to estimate the military genius of Marlborough, or the literary genius of Swift. Devoutly attached to the Church of England, simple in her habits, decorous in her life, she never showed any power, and seldom any wish, to comprehend the great issues of European politics, the fierce struggles of political parties, which were decided and fought out by her soldiers and ministers in her name. In religion narrow, constant, and sincere, she gave the rest of her small mind to determining the rival claims of her favourites upon her preference and her affections. If she had been born to a private station, she would have passed almost unnoticed as a good woman and a regular churchgoer, with a singular incapacity for rearing the numerous children to whom she gave birth. The tempests that rocked the world in which, from no choice of her own, she played a conspicuous, if not an important, part, scarcely stirred the dull shallows of her soul. Greatness, in the vulgar sense of the word, was thrust upon her, but it only made her wretched. In obscurity she might have been happy. She would never have been remarkable for intellect or character.

Anne's parentage was illustrious in more than the heraldic sense. Of her two grandfathers, one would have been thought by all men capable of reigning if he had never reigned, and the other wrote books which are still read with delight by all lovers of good literature, or of history at first hand. Charles the First had some kingly qualities, among them the fatal belief that a King of England could be above the law. Of art and letters he was a careful student, and an excellent judge. His Chancellor of the Exchequer, Edward Hyde, afterwards Earl of Clarendon, the father of Queen Anne's mother, was a man of high character and great abilities, an honour to the Royalist cause, and to the profession of letters. His Autobiography, still more than his Rebellion, has a permanent fascination even for those readers who look upon the Long Parliament as the saviour of English freedom.

Queen Anne's father has achieved an unenviable fame as the worst of English sovereigns, and the redeeming features in his character are not easy to discover. He had a real love of cruelty, and his heart was pronounced by Marlborough, who knew him well, to be as hard as marble. The private character of Charles the First was beyond reproach. James the Second was in youth almost as dissolute as his elder brother, but his taste in women was such that the Merry Monarch described his brother's mistresses as given him by his confessors in penance for his sins. Although James Stuart and George Jeffreys endeavoured, when their crimes had landed both of them in ruin and disgrace, to throw the blame for their united wickedness upon each other, there is quite enough for the two, nor is it necessary to settle the proportions of public iniquity between them. When James secretly married Anne Hyde in 1660, he was still a Protestant. He was Duke of York, and heir presumptive to the throne. His father-in-law had been Prince Charles's titular Chancellor since 1658, and received the Great Seal at the Restoration, with the title which his books have made for ever famous. The Duke of York became Lord High Admiral, and, as we know from the diary of Samuel Pepys, was assiduous in the discharge of his official duties. As a soldier or sailor, he might have won credit, if not distinction. As a civil servant he would not perhaps have risen to the top of the tree. But he would have earned by laborious and methodical diligence his salary, his pension, and the approval of his superiors. He had also, it must be admitted, that parsimonious economy which, disagreeable as it may be in private life, is a shining virtue in public men. That he did not find out Mr. Pepys's defalcations, which were unknown till the recent discovery of that ingenious gentleman's most secret cipher, only proves that Pepys was a good deal cleverer in manipulating figures than His Royal Highness. James's first wife has left no mark upon history, though her features have been preserved on the canvas of Lely. She had been before her marriage maid of honour to the Princess of Orange, and it was at Buda that she met James, then, like his brother, in exile. Of her children only two survived childhood, but they became successively Queens of England. Anne, the younger, was born at St. James's Palace on the 6th of February, 1665, and educated in the religion of her parents, then both members of the National Church. The reaction against Puritanism was at its height. Charles the Second, though his natural abilities were great, far greater than the abilities of James, detested all business, loved only pleasure, and hated only to be bored. His one settled determination was that never again, to use his own words, would he "go on his travels." His desire was to govern, so far as possible, without a Parliament, and to put himself under the protection of the French King. His patriotism, so far as he had any, was hampered by his vices, and his courtiers taught him to believe that Oliver Cromwell, "the greatest Prince who ever ruled England," who made the name of England honoured by every Protestant, and dreaded by every Catholic, Power, was an execrable traitor. "Charles the First," says Junius, with rhetorical exaggeration, "lived and died a hypocrite. Charles the Second was a hypocrite of another sort, and should have died upon the same scaffold." He died in his bed, with the courtesy and good humour that seldom failed him. But long before his death he had thrown away the fruits of Cromwell's victories, and made England contemptible. By the infamous Treaty of Dover, signed and sealed in 1670, he had "bound himself to make public profession of the Roman Catholic religion, to join his armies to those of Louis for the purpose of destroying the power of the United Provinces, and to employ the whole strength of England, by land and sea, in support of the rights of the House of Bourbon to the vast monarchy of Spain." In return for these degrading promises Charles the Second obtained from Louis the Fourteenth a large annual dole, and a guarantee of support against his own subjects if they were driven to rebellion. Well might Charles Fox say that the worst of all revolutions was a restoration.

Charles the Second, who never had any real religion, was for proclaiming himself a Roman Catholic at once. His more prudent ally, who had taken care to become acquainted with English opinion, and knew that the Protestantism of the English people was incorrigible, induced him to practise for the time a hypocritical concealment, and to attend the services of the Church of England. One service was the same as another to Charles, if only the sermon were short. He went to church as seldom as he decently could, and usually provided himself with a plentiful supply of light literature, in case the sermon should be long. He even took the sacrament in both kinds, and on account of his politic acquiescence the Pope refused him till the last moment admittance into the Church of Rome. His brother James was less compliant. It is probable that James had already become a Roman Catholic, and at all events he warmly supported the Treaty of Dover. He was in his way a religious man. Morally far worse than his brother, for he was cruel as well as licentious, he did put himself under the priests with a thoroughness that left nothing to be desired. His religion may be called superstition,, for it had no influence upon his morality, and was as far as possible removed from the teaching of Christ. But, such as it was, it was genuine, and he adhered to it at all costs for the rest of his life. After the Treaty of Dover he ceased to appear in the Royal Chapel. The law as it then stood did not exclude a Catholic from succession to the throne, and by a declaration of doubtful legality the King dispensed Catholics from the penal laws against them. In 1673, however, the Test Act was passed, and the Duke of York found himself under the necessity of abjuring the Catholic faith, or resigning his office as Lord High Admiral. He resigned; though eleven years afterwards he was permitted, by a flagrant illegality, to take his place again at the Board. His two daughters, by express command of his brother, were brought up to be Protestants. For Charles, who was no fool, perceived clearly enough that if, in a matter for which he was responsible, the Church of Rome were given precedence over the Church of England, the secret article of the Treaty of Dover, that which concerned his own religion, might as well be published in the Gazette. Anne, Duchess of York, had been received with her husband into communion with Rome. But she died in 1671, and her husband married Mary of Modena in 1673, This open union with a Catholic Princess increased an unpopularity which required no augmentation, and was even censured by the House of Commons. "My dear James," said Charles, on receiving from his brother some hint about the danger of assassination, "they will never kill me to make you King." James, however, bigoted as he was, did not attempt to interfere with the education of Anne.

Left motherless when she was only eight years old, the little Princess Anne formed after a time an affectionate attachment to Sarah Jennings, a girl five years older than herself, whose strong will and violent temper gradually and completely dominated her own. On the 23rd of January, 1676, at the age of thirteen, she was confirmed in the Church of England by Henry Compton, Bishop of London, who had been a cornet in the Horse Guards, and was said by her father to talk more like a colonel than a bishop. He was undoubtedly a pugnacious personage, and a vehement antagonist of the Roman Church. Thus all Anne's surroundings at the most impressionable period of her life were Protestant, and her religious estrangement from her father was complete. Her sister Mary was married at fifteen to William, Prince of Orange, then twenty-seven, the greatest statesman in Europe, a staunch Protestant, and the sworn enemy from boyhood to the magnificent King of France. Anne's own marriage was much discussed. The Elector of Hanover, afterwards George the First, was a suitor for her hand. Her own predilection was for John Sheffield, Earl of Mulgrave, whom she called Jack. But her personal leanings were set at nought, the Act of Settlement was not anticipated, and in 1683, being then eighteen, she became the wife of a Lutheran Prince, George of Denmark, brother of King Christian the Fifth, What Pope falsely said of most women is perfectly true of Prince George. He had no character at all. So many things surprised him, that his favourite ejaculation was Est-il possible? He seemed to care for nothing but his dinner and his bottle. Charles the Second, a pretty shrewd judge of men, said, "I have tried Prince George sober, and I have tried him drunk. Drunk or sober, there is nothing in him."

Far more important than her marriage in the life of Anne, as in the history of Europe, was the appointment of her old playfellow Sarah Jennings, now Lady Churchill, to be her woman of the bedchamber. For Lady Churchill's husband was the first soldier of his age, if indeed as a soldier he has ever in any age been surpassed.

The later career of this extraordinary man, with its shining magnificence and its shameless treason, fills the public stage during the reign of Queen Anne. When the old connection between his wife and the young Princess became official in 1683, he had been for a year Baron Churchill of Aymouth in the peerage of Scotland. While he was page to the Duke of York, who seduced his sister, Arabella Churchill, and befriended him in consequence, he had fascinated one of the King's favourites, the Duchess of Cleveland, by his handsome looks. The result was in one particular unusual. For the Duchess gave her lover a large sum of money, and he invested it on the best landed security without scruple or delay. Few are the young men of real life who have profited in a financial sense by their vices, like Tom Jones and Porthos in fiction. But John Churchill was an exception to most rules. A miserly soldier is not common. Churchill's love of money amounted to a passion, and for better for worse, for richer for poorer, he clung to it throughout his life. What Macaulay well describes as his "far-sighted, sure-footed judgment" kept him true to his own interests, and eager for his own promotion, alike in youth and in manhood, when he was the unknown son of a penniless courtier, and when the sovereigns of Europe were his obedient suitors. Of fidelity and of friendship he seemed almost incapable. Yet there were two points on which his conduct is absolutely beyond criticism or reproach. He was the staunchest of Protestants. Notwithstanding his lawful and unlawful relations with James, the most devout of Catholics, he never would hear of changing his religion.

The other point is more closely connected with the subject of this book. When he was twenty-eight, and a colonel of foot, he fell in love with Sarah Jennings, a high-spirited girl of eighteen, with a "fury temper, and a fairy face"; and, though she had not a penny, he married her. From that moment she was the only human being that he either loved or feared. The intimacy between his wife and the Princess was not affected by the marriage of either. They called each other by pet names. Anne was Mrs. Morley, Sarah was Mrs. Freeman. The ascendency of Mrs. Freeman over Mrs. Morley, of a strong character over a weak one, grew absolute by degrees. It must be remembered that at this time, in 1683, the probability of Anne becoming Queen was just one of those nice calculations on which a mind like Churchill's loves to dwell. The King was only fifty-three, but he had severely tried his constitution by his excesses, and he had no legitimate children. His brother was three years younger, and Mary of Modena, the second Duchess of York, might at any time have a son. Anne's sister, the Princess of Orange, stood before her in the succession. But her husband was Stadtholder of Holland, and it was conceivable that on that account the Parliament of England might pass her over. A Bill to exclude the Duke of York from the throne on account of his creed had passed the House of Commons in 1680. Misled by the genius of George Savile, Marquess of Halifax, a consummate debater, but a man more witty than wise, the Lords rejected it, and thus prepared the way for the most disastrous reign in English history, with the possible exception of Mary Tudor's. But a Bill which had already passed one House might in future pass both Houses, and receive the Royal Assent, so that the succession of James was not secure until, on the 6th of February, 1685, Charles the Second died after a short illness, having first been received into the Church of Rome, and confessed himself to a Roman priest.

Churchill was at the outset a faithful subject of the new Sovereign. He went on an embassy to Paris for a renewal of the disgraceful subsidy which Charles had received from Louis, and he was created an English peer for his pains. He took a part, though a subordinate part, in putting down the rebellion of Monmouth, Charles's natural son, at Sedgemoor. But this strange man's conscience was as uneasy as his convictions were unsettled. Difficult as it may be to reconcile some incidents of his life with the precepts or practice of any religion, there can be no doubt that he was sincerely attached to the Protestant Church of England. He had, moreover, many sources of information, his judgment was almost infallible, and he soon perceived that James's tenure of the throne was much less stable than his wife's hold upon Princess Anne, while, if James remained King, the position of no Protestant would be secure. He was not in the habit of allowing other people to profit by his knowledge. When James declared open war upon Protestantism by turning Protestants out of their places, Churchill entered into treasonable correspondence with William of Orange. Through Lady Churchill he was sure of the Princess. So far as Anne understood politics, and had a will of her own, she was a Tory, and a believer in divine right. But her mind was almost as limited as her husband's, and on most points her will was the will of Sarah Churchill. Her isolation helped to rivet the chain. She deserted the cause of her father, who had shown her very little affection, and accepted William the Deliverer, her brother-in-law, as her rightful Protestant sovereign. Mary was childless. Anne herself had borne several children, who all died in infancy. While the Revolution was being actively prepared, on the 10th of June, 1688, James the Second's son, known with familiar contempt as the "Old Pretender," made his appearance in the world. The "warming-pan" story has been long since exploded, and no one now questions the legitimacy of this child. But his birth appeared too opportune for rational belief, it was surrounded by the Court with a foolish secrecy, and an irrational incredulity prevailed throughout the ranks of Protestant Whigs. In any case it was too late to draw back. James persisted in his lawless oppression, and on the anniversary of the Gunpowder Plot William landed at Torbay. Anne fully believed that the child called James Stuart was supposititious. Otherwise, she thought, she would herself have been summoned to her stepmother's bedside; whereas she was in fact made the victim of practical jokes, and sent on a wild-goose chase, which naturally mystified her, and made her suspect foul play. She was fond of her sister, and the knowledge that Mary would be, at least in name, a reigning Queen helped to reconcile her to the Revolution. On the nth of April, 1689, she attended the coronation of William and Mary. She soon found that her sister's Queenship was a mere fiction. Mary was the most submissive of women, and William was the proudest of men. He had not left his beloved Holland, for which his heart always yearned, to be his wife's gentleman usher. Although Mary was legally Queen, Parliament had given the power, as distinguished from the title, of Sovereign exclusively to him, and he was not even in all respects minded to be a constitutional King. The example of James was indeed quite sufficient to prevent him from overriding, or attempting to override, the law. He treated the House of Commons with punctilious respect. But he had not the modern idea of acting upon the advice of his Ministers, nor of changing them on account of a Parliamentary vote. A master of European statecraft, he determined to be his own Minister for Foreign Affairs, nor was there any one of his subjects who would so well have discharged the duties. Churchill was in 1689 created Earl of Marlborough, and was invested on various occasions with important commands. But William never trusted him, and he is said to have been the one man before whom that intrepid spirit quailed.

Late in the summer of 1689 was born the only one of Anne's numerous children who survived babyhood. This little boy was created Duke of Gloucester by William, who petted him, and gave him in charge to Marlborough for his military education, saying: "Make him like yourself." At last it appeared as if the succession to the throne were established, and for some years to come nothing was said about the House of Hanover. But though William, in his cold, dry way, was kind to his wife's small nephew, the Princess Anne was not on the best of terms with the King and Queen. The great King, who was never popular with his subjects, had no charm of manner, and no superficial accomplishments. His noble character, his dauntless courage, and his profound intelligence, were the objects of his wife's idolatrous admiration, though as a husband he had at first given her good reason to be jealous of the gifted Elizabeth Villiers, afterwards Countess of Orkney, called by Swift the wisest woman he ever knew. Anne was quite incapable of appreciating or understanding him. In her familiar correspondence with her "Mrs. Freeman" she called him "Caliban, alias the Dutch Monster." Mary could not endure any disrespect shown to William, and her devotion succeeded at last in winning his heart, so that they became an absolutely united couple. When, in conversation about her allowance, Anne talked of appealing to her friends, Mary said tartly, "Pray, what friends have you but the King and me?" She disliked the moody silence and the sullen temper of her sister, so different from her own vivacious gaiety, Anne's income was raised, after some demur, from thirty to fifty thousand pounds a year, much of which probably went to the Churchills. But her estrangement from the Court was increased by the King's most wise refusal to employ Prince George in any public situation, and completed on the 21st of January, 1692, by the sudden dismissal of Lord Marlborough from all the offices he held. For this step on the King's part there was ample ground. Marlborough was in secret and treacherous correspondence with the exile of St. Germains. He was seeking to influence English opinion against the Dutch favourites of the King, especially Bentinck, and he was quite prepared to assist, if it became necessary, for his own purposes in the conditional restoration of James. Legal proof against him may not then have been forthcoming, and the strongest, though certainly not the sole, evidence is supplied by the posthumous Memoirs of James himself. But William knew a great deal, if not everything, and Marlborough was far too dangerous an enemy to be treated with indulgence, or with contempt. Anne shared the fate of the Marlboroughs, and left the Court with them. To live without her precious Mrs. Freeman was impossible for her. With Mrs. Freeman she was always happy, and her husband was always happy with his bottle. So matters remained until Queen Mary died of smallpox, the great scourge of the age, on the 28th of December, 1694. She was only thirty-four, and her death was quite unexpected. Indeed, it had been pretty generally assumed that she would survive her husband, marry again, and have children who would destroy all chance of Anne's succession to the throne. Anne was now by the Bill of Rights the heir presumptive. She had a son living. The revival or continuance of the Stuart dynasty might come through her, and at all events, when she succeeded to the throne, Marlborough would be the most powerful person in the State. He ceased to engage in Jacobite plots, and actively sought through the Princess Anne a reconciliation with the Court. William was the most placable of men. It was always from policy that he acted, being devoid alike of cruelty and of fear. After her sister's death Anne was again treated with the ceremonious honour appropriate to her rank, which had been, after her quarrel with Mary, withheld from her, and in 1698 Marlborough recovered his position, not because the King had ceased to distrust him, but because William's clear intellect perceived the change in the situation, which destroyed Marlborough's motive for treason.

The little Duke of Gloucester, though he had a small cannon and a tiny regiment of his own, was not left exclusively to Marlborough. Bishop Burnet instructed him in history, and was delighted with a progress which may have been forced. At any rate, the child of so many hopes did not enter his twelfth year. When he died at the age of eleven, on the 30th of July, 1700, the ultimate succession to the Crown was again in jeopardy. After so many disappointments, belief in Anne as a mother had ceased, and it became necessary that Parliament should make provision for the future of the State. Such was the origin of the famous Act of Settlement, which received William's assent on the 12th of June, 1701. By this statute the Crown of England devolved upon Anne after the death of the King, and, in the event of her dying without further issue, upon the Electress Sophia of Hanover, granddaughter of James the First. A few months after the House of Hanover had thus been introduced into English history James the Second died at St. Germains. Before the breath was out of James's body, the French monarch, whose treatment of the royal exile had always been extremely generous, had, with singular imprudence, assured the dying man that his son should be recognised as James the Third of England. The English people were deeply and justly incensed and alarmed. The Pretender was at once attainted. Men and money were voted for military operations against France. The Abjuration Bill, requiring all persons who held any public office to abjure the pretensions of James Stuart, was hurried through Parliament.

William the Third lived just long enough to give this Act his sanction. On the 8th of March, 1702, he died of internal injuries caused by the stumble of a horse, and Anne became Queen of England. Marlborough could not have hoped for a more favourable conjunction of circumstances. His old master James was no longer alive to reproach or incriminate him. The very different King who had just passed away was almost the only person he could not beguile or deceive. The new Queen was the obedient slave of his wife. The opening of a great campaign on the Continent of Europe against the first Catholic power of the world called for a Protestant general of military genius, or, in other words, for the Earl of Marlborough. His various treacheries were not known as they are known now. He had had the good fortune to be once falsely accused by an unprincipled adventurer, and the victim of a forgery is always sure of a strong presumption in favour of his general innocence. Marlborough entered under the best auspices upon the most glorious phase of his life.

On the 23rd of April, St. George's Day, Anne was crowned in accordance with the Act of Settlement, and the reign of the Churchills began. The Earl of Marlborough was made a Duke, and Captain General of her Majesty's forces, with an annual pension of five thousand pounds, settled upon him for the Queen's life. The Duchess became Mistress of the Robes. Godolphin, a man of Marlborough's own choice, received the appointment of Lord Treasurer, to whom the First Lord of the Treasury is the nearest modern approximation. "Sidney Godolphin," said Charles the Second, whom he served in various offices, "Sidney Godolphin is never in the way, and never out of the way." Godolphin was a man of low character, low aims, low tastes and pursuits. He had corresponded with James while he was in the service of William, and he had always been ready to join Marlborough in any proposed intrigue. He cared nothing for literature, or for science, or indeed for anything except politics and sport. But he was an industrious man of business, and an expert administrator, who knew every turn of the machine, and every move of the game. If he had any principles, he was a Tory. His real leader was Marlborough, whom he served with as much fidelity as he was capable of showing to any one. It was legally imperative that Parliament should be dissolved within six months of King William's death, and the general election of 1702 produced a large Tory majority. This result well suited Anne. Her Toryism was genuine, so genuine indeed that it made her uncomfortable about her own position. She could not be sure that "James the Third," though he might be a Pretender, was not the legitimate son of her father and her stepmother. Could his religion exclude him from the throne? A Whig would say that that was & question for Parliament, which had decided it against the Pretender. A Tory was in the days of the Exclusion Bill, and to some extent was still, a man or woman who believed in divine right. Anne could scarcely help asking in her heart of hearts whether this boy of fourteen was not lawful King of England, Scotland, and Ireland. Probably the Churchills quieted her fears. The Duke and Duchess were not troubled with many scruples. But Protestants they were, and they held it a duty to deliver the country from Papists. They could easily represent to Anne that if she were to abdicate. Parliament would at once send for the Electress Sophia, and that her brother James would not have the slightest chance of taking her place. They could appeal, no doubt they did appeal, to her love for the Church of England, which was deep and sincere. But whatever Mrs. Freeman wanted, Mrs. Morley would readily give her, even to the half of her kingdom. As Captain General of the Forces, Marlborough was pre-eminently in his right place. Louis was still bent upon the restoration of a Catholic King in England, and the death of William had encouraged his hopes. England was committed to a great war, and stood in need of her great General to cope with the Marshals of France. In her first speech to the Privy Council, where her musical voice was much admired, the Queen announced that the country with its allies would "oppose the great power of France." Some offence was caused, though it is unlikely that any was meant, by her protest on the same occasion that her heart was entirely English. This was thought to be a reflection upon her predecessor, whose heart was entirely Dutch, and who had placed his head alone at the service of his adopted country. But Anne had a Danish husband, who spoke the French language, and it is unnecessary to look for hidden meanings in a phrase of perfectly natural sentiment. Prince George had been created Duke of Cumberland, and was entitled to sit in the House of Lords, where he duly took his seat. An annuity of a hundred thousand a year was secured to him in case he survived the Queen, who was ten years younger than himself. Otherwise he received no increase of dignity, and continued to be, as he always had been, a cipher in public affairs. "One good trooper would have been a greater loss," said King James on hearing that he had been deserted by Prince George.

When Marlborough received his Dukedom, he was fifty-two, and in the full enjoyment of all his magnificent powers. In the summer of 1702 he left England to command the allied forces on the Continent, and established his head-quarters at Nimeguen on the Rhine in Holland. War with France had been declared in May, and was at that time popular with both parties in the State, except with those logically consistent Tories who were also Jacobites. For, though it carried out the policy of William, and was to that extent a Whig war, it was national because directed against the French King, who had presumed to dictate the devolution of the British Crown. Marlborough had learned the art of soldiering under Turenne. But he was not in the least reluctant to turn against the French the lessons they had unconsciously taught him. The head of the Ministry, Godolphin, was at that time a Tory. Marlborough was ostensibly sometimes a Tory and sometimes a Whig. In truth and in fact he was neither one nor the other. He disliked "party heats," and party government, then in its infancy, did not appeal to his cool, subtle, calculating mind.

Unhappily religious discord was rife not merely between Catholics and Protestants, but among Protestants themselves. The toleration of Dissenters, who were Whigs almost to a man, was thoroughly displeasing to the High Churchmen, who were without exception Tories. The Queen sympathised with these "Highflyers," as they were called, but she was rather embarrassed by the fact that her own husband was a Lutheran Protestant, not in communion with the Church of England. The High Churchmen could not very well get at Prince George. A man of genius was an easier prey. Daniel Defoe had not yet become immortal as the author of Robinson Crusoe, and he was little known to fame. Dissenters at that time, and for more than a hundred years afterwards, were incapable of holding office without taking the sacrament according to the rites of the Established Church. It was even proposed to go further against them, and by an Occasional Conformity Bill, that is a Bill against occasional conformity, to exclude them from civil employment altogether at the very time when Louis the Fourteenth, having crushed Protestantism in France, was seeking to crush it in England. Defoe, assuming the character of a High Churchman, gravely recommended that Nonconformists should be exterminated. This proposal, called the Shortest Way with the Dissenters, is a masterpiece of savage irony, not unworthy of Swift. It did its work too well for the author's own ease and comfort. Hundreds of readers were taken in, and supposed that they had before them the genuine pamphlet of a Tory zealot. Those High Churchmen who understood the stratagem did not see the joke. They called upon the Government to prosecute the author, and in July 1703, seven months after the publication of the tract, Defoe was sentenced to imprisonment, as well as to exposure on the pillory. He stood on that bad eminence in Cornhill, in Cheapside, and at Temple Bar. The people did not share the folly of their rulers. They gathered round him, not to pelt him, nor abuse him, but to cheer him, and to drink his health. In November he was released from gaol on the intercession of Robert Harley, afterwards Earl of Oxford, then Speaker of the House of Commons. Defoe came out of prison to find his business as a manufacturer ruined. But Harley appreciated his literary talents, and the value of his services. The alliance between them was for the mutual benefit of both, and Harley owed more to Defoe than Defoe owed to Harley. For years after Harley's admission to the Cabinet he was a regular spy in the pay of the Government, although, as the Portland Papers show, he often complained to Harley of his inadequate remuneration.

Defoe regained his liberty just in time to describe, with his inimitably graphic power, the storm which swept over England at the end of November 1703, the most terrible that has visited this island within recorded times. The loss of life was considerable. The loss of property was immense. On the estate of John Evelyn, the Diarist, two thousand trees were destroyed. Ships were sunk by the score. London and Bristol looked as if they had been taken by storm. The Palace at Wells collapsed, and crushed the Bishop, Dr. Kidder, who had succeeded the saintly non-juror Ken. Parliament voted an Address to the Crown, and a general fast was ordered by the Queen. There were as many people in mourning as if a great battle had been fought. The House of Commons intervened, not merely on general grounds of sympathy with the public distress, but also because so many of her Majesty's ships had been ruined that it became necessary to make better provision for maintaining the strength of the fleet.

The last Parliament of William the Third left to the first Parliament of Anne the legacy of a constitutional struggle between the two Houses, which arose out of the celebrated Aylesbury case, known to lawyers as Ashby v. White. Aylesbury was one of the boroughs which enjoyed the widest possible suffrage for men long before the days of Parliamentary reform. The House of Commons, which at that time, and for more than a hundred and fifty years afterwards, claimed to be the sole authority in determining the legal right to vote, had declared the franchise of Aylesbury to be vested in all adult male inhabitants not maintained by parochial relief. A poor ostler named Ashby, then just above the line, though he soon sank below it, tendered his vote to White, the Constable acting on behalf of the Sheriff, which White refused to accept. That White broke the law was clear. The question was what remedy belonged to the disfranchised Ashby. Having put himself, it may be presumed, in the hands of some local attorney, Ashby brought an action against White at the Aylesbury Assizes, and recovered five pounds by way of damages. This simple proceeding on his part, or on the part of his backers, shook the fabric of the Constitution. His antagonist White, the defendant in the cause, applied to the Court of Queen's Bench for an order to set aside the verdict as bad in law upon the admitted facts. The Lord Chief Justice of that Court in those days was a very great and famous personage. Sir John Holt. Holt ranks among the sages of the law, and is honoured for having taken a leading part in raising the judicial bench from the discredit into which it had fallen before the Revolution. But on this occasion he was outvoted by his colleagues, and the Court decided against his opinion by three to one that Ashby had suffered no tort, no actionable wrong, for the reason, among others, that the candidates of his choice had both been elected. From this judgment the poor ostler, through his attorney, or the attorney through his poor ostler, appealed to the House of Lords. The Lords, not the Law Lords, but the whole House, reversed it, and then the trouble began. For the peers had presumed to meddle with an election to the House of Commons. By this time William the Third had died, Anne was on the throne, another House of Commons had been chosen, and Ashby was a pauper in receipt of public alms. But a great issue was at stake, and everything was forgotten except the rival jealousies of Lords and Commons. The indirect control exercised by one House over the other was very great, for many peers owned pocket boroughs, and many pocket boroughs belonged to the same peer. All the more did the Commons think it requisite to protest against the direct influence of the hereditary Chamber. When Ashby took out execution, he was ordered into the custody of the Serjeant-at-arms. The Serjeant was further directed to find and bring to the bar the counsel and attorneys who had brought the case before the Lords. The Lords resolved that they should be set at liberty. Their Lordships then, perceiving that the quarrel had reached a stage which could not be called dignified, desired a Conference with the Commons in the Painted Chamber. The Conference was held, but it did not bring peace. For the Commons took the opportunity to protest by way of recrimination against the novel practice of bringing appeals from the Court of Chancery to the House of Lords, who had hitherto confined themselves to determining, as in the present case, writs of error at common law. The Lords therefore broke off the Conference, and the dispute might have become really serious if the Queen had not interrupted it by the simple process of proroguing Parliament. This sensible course, for which Godolphin was responsible, put an end to the matter, and it was never revived. Historians, too contemptuous, and perhaps sometimes too ignorant, of the law, have represented the Lords as vindicators of electoral right. But to argue thus is to miss the true point, which was not the wrong, but the remedy. If Ashby had petitioned the House of Commons, the decision of the Constable would have been set aside, and the vote would have been allowed. The suffrage was not given him as a material possession on which he could set a pecuniary value, but as a political privilege to be used for public purposes alone. No legal tribunal had any right to a voice in the question, which was exclusively for the House of Commons. It is only by statutes passed long after Anne's reign that the judges have acquired rights which Holt most properly disclaimed.

In 1705 another great constitutional change was made, and made, as all such changes should be, by Act of Parliament. During William the Third's reign there had been unsuccessful attempts to exclude all placemen from the House of Commons. If these efforts had succeeded, the House of Commons would have been deprived of active participation in the government of the country, and would have lost control over the Ministers of the Crown. Such a disability was long afterwards inserted in the Constitution of the United States by the political philosophers who drew up that famous instrument, and the result has been to make the American Cabinet little more than clerks under the orders of the President. The statute of Anne, which, though modified, has never been repealed, enacts that no one holding an office of profit under the Crown which was not in existence on the 25th of October, 1705, shall sit in the House of Commons, and that the acceptance by a Member of that House of an office which did then exist shall vacate his seat, though he may be re-elected. If his office has been created since that day, he is disqualified for election, unless of course he be expressly qualified by the Act which establishes the post, or by some later statute. The broad result of this legislation, and the rules framed in accordance with it for the discipline of the public service, is that political officers may, and practically must, sit in the Legislature, while permanent members of the Civil Service are excluded from Parliament altogether. From 1705 to 1867 every member of Parliament who accepted an office of profit under the Crown vacated his seat, and submitted himself, if eligible, for re-election, even though he passed in due course from the Solicitor to the Attorney-Generalship. In 1867 it was provided that transference from one office to another should not create a vacancy. By this rough and ready method, illogical, inartistic, and practically sound, two great and paramount objects are achieved. In the first place the Cabinet, the governing body of the Empire, is entirely composed from the two Houses of Parliament, and constantly associated with them. In the second place, the Civil Service, upon which Ministers of all parties alike depend, is kept free from controversial strife, and is confined to the sole business of efficient administration.

The Queen, who believed in divine right, took little interest in constitutional questions, except so far as they affected the Church of England. To that Church she gave in commemoration of her thirty-ninth birthday, which fell upon the 6th of February, 1704, a splendid present, ever since called by her name, and known as Queen Anne's Bounty. The First Fruits and Tenths, being a charge upon land, originally levied for ecclesiastical purposes, had been diverted from the Roman to the English Court by Henry the Eighth. Charles the Second could find no better use for them than to make provision for his favourites and their children. Bishop Burnet, a staunch Churchman, though a friend of Dissenters, and a fervent Whig, had tried hard in the previous reign to procure this fund for the small benefices of the Church. Where he had failed with William he succeeded with Anne. The assent of Parliament was obtained, and the statutes of mortmain were so far repealed, that bequests to the particular corporation which had charge of this fund became by statute legal. Two circumstances, however, postponed and hampered the beneficial operation of Queen Anne's Bounty. The charges upon it were not cleared off until the Queen and Burnet were both in their graves. But long after that date, 1715, long after 1815, the other and more serious hindrance continued to operate. The amount of a benefice was no guide to the means of the incumbent. For he might, and often did, hold other preferments besides, putting in curates to do the work for which he received the stipend. To reform the Church of England in 1704, or in 1804, would have been considered sacrilegious. The Establishment was still the rich man's Church, and it was not the poorest parsons who, before the year 1838, derived most benefit from the bounty of Queen Anne.

Lord Godolphin, though not a free trader in the modern and scientific sense of the term, was too good a man of business to neglect the vast importance of international trade. By the Methuen Treaty with Portugal, signed at Lisbon in December 1703, and called after the British Minister accredited to the Portuguese Court, the woollen manufactures of England were admitted into King Pedro's dominions, and the British Government on the other hand agreed that the duty on Portuguese wine should always be less by one-third than the duty on the wine of France. Accustomed as we are to see such taxes regulated not by place of origin, but by degree of alcoholic strength, we may feel surprised at a measure so little likely to promote the cause of temperance as the encouragement of port at the expense of claret. It appears, however, that burgundy, rather than bordeaux, was the favourite drink with the wealthier classes at the beginning of the eighteenth century and there is more gout in burgundy than there is in port. If we turn to the opposite side of the treaty, the extension of the woollen trade, it may be said with fairness of this commercial instrument, which diminished taxation and opened markets, that England gave nothing which was not for her advantage, and yet received a premium for what she gave. The effect upon the habits of Englishmen was not immediate; and William Murray, Lord Mansfield, born in 1705, "drank champagne," sweet champagne, "with the wits," including Pope. But the supremacy of port, which may be said to have culminated with the younger Pitt, to whom it was first medicine and then poison, had its origin in the Methuen Treaty of 1703.

At the time, however, the political rather than the commercial aspect of the treaty engrossed public attention. The War of the Spanish Succession had already begun. Louis the Fourteenth had put forward as his candidate for the throne of Spain his own grandson, Philip, Duke of Anjou, second son of the Dauphin. Portugal favoured the claims of the Austrian Archduke Charles, which were adopted by this country to preserve the balance of power from the overweening ambition of the French King. England, freedom, and Protestantism, which are almost convertible terms, never had, not even in Napoleon, a more dangerous enemy than the vain and cruel bigot who then governed France. By revoking the Edict of Nantes Louis and Madame de Maintenon had made war upon the Protestant faith. By acknowledging the Pretender as King of England the King of France made war upon the English people. By assuming to treat the throne of Spain as an appanage of the House of Bourbon, he claimed universal dominion in Europe. The death of William the Third had removed from his path the statesman best qualified to baffle French diplomacy. Now the appeal was to arms, and there stepped forward as the English champion, in the hour of need, a figure of surpassing splendour. Enough has been said to show that the character of John Churchill, Duke of Marlborough, was neither pure nor high. He was not truthful. He was not straightforward. He was not honest. In his love of money, and his capacity for hoarding it, he rivalled those wretched misers who have done no more than contemplate their gains. And yet, such are the strange freaks in which nature indulges, this mean and selfish intriguer was endowed with perfect courage, with an irresistible charm of manner, with a temper which even his wife failed to disturb, with a brain that no sophistry could obscure, and with a military genius before which criticism is humbly silent. Lord Chesterfield, whose taste has become proverbial, and w-hose intellect was far stronger than those who know him only through his letters would suppose, pronounced that the graces were absorbed by the Duke of Marlborough. As fearless as William of Orange, and not less able, he succeeded where the King failed, and failed where the King succeeded. No one ever doubted William's word. The keenest Jacobites acknowledged in their candid moments that he was a just and merciful man. Moral confidence was a feeling which Marlborough never, except in battle, inspired. He was treacherous even for a treacherous age. Wholly devoid of cruelty, and by nature humane, he is said never to have sacrificed an unnecessary life. But he used his fellow-creatures for his own purposes, and when he had no further use for them, he forgot their existence. He made his plans and carried them out with the absolute efficiency of sheer intelligence and the serene implacability of impersonal fate. There are incidents of his career which make it impossible to credit him with a disinterested patriotism. Happily for England, it was his interest to be patriotic after the deaths of James and William. The Pretender, though Marlborough characteristically kept on good terms with him through his natural brother, his own nephew, Berwick, was not after 1702 a serious object to the first soldier in Europe, the husband of the favourite of the Queen. What was Marlborough's personal religion we are not to inquire. These things are secrets between man and his Maker. But here again fortune favoured England. For Protestantism, the right of private judgment, the freedom of the layman from the priest, Marlborough was at all periods of his life ready to contend. Even his devotion to the Church of England, though very different in kind from the Queen's, was apparently not less sincere, and had resisted all the seductions of her father. He was now the hope of England, and of the Protestant alliance, as the King of France was their sworn foe.

The object of Louis and his Marshals in the spring of 1704 was to carry the war into the heart of the enemy's country by attacking Vienna. The Elector of Bavaria, faithless to the cause of the Empire, was ready to help them. With the Elector was Marshal Marsin. Marshal Tallard entered the Black Forest in May to reinforce them both. Marlborough made up his mind that the French should never reach Vienna. After much tiresome negotiation with the States General of Holland, in which his tact and dexterity prevailed over Dutch jealousy and weakness, he left the Hague for Coblentz on the 5th of May. From Coblentz he marched to Mayence, and then, after crossing the Neckar, he met at Mindelheim Prince Eugene, a Savoyard born in Paris, and now in command of the Austrian armies. Although his name has been eclipsed by Marlborough's, Eugene was a great general, and took his share in the mighty victories by which the pride of Louis was humbled to the dust. Entire friendship and concord were always maintained between these illustrious commanders. With them was joined on this occasion, a man much inferior to either, Prince Louis of Baden, who would not acquiesce in Marlborough's supremacy, and could not be restrained from taking part in the Bavarian campaign. While Prince Eugene moved to defend Baden against Tallard, Marlborough, accompanied against his will by Louis, crossed the Alps at Gieslingen, and proceeded by Ulm to Donauwerth, where there was a bridge across the

Danube. To occupy Donauwerth, however, it was necessary that he should first take possession of the Schellenberg, a hill which rose gradually, and overhung the town. By an absurd arrangement, which the great general accepted because it was inevitable, Marlborough and Prince Louis commanded on alternate days. The second of July was Marlborough's day, and he directed that the Schellenberg should be stormed. His orders were carried out by the English foot after two unsuccessful efforts, with the assistance of their German allies, and the Bavarians fled in confusion, leaving sixteen pieces of artillery behind them. The English losses were heavy. But Marlborough's object had been accomplished. Instead of marching triumphantly on Vienna, as he otherwise would have done, the Elector of Bavaria was compelled to fall back upon Augsburg. Marlborough established himself at Donauwerth, and Bavaria lay at his disposal. He offered terms to the Elector, and it was not until they were refused that he ordered the country round Munich to be laid waste. He was by nature mild and placable. He did nothing contrary to the laws of war as then understood. He was simply bent upon bringing the campaign to a successful issue in the shortest possible time.

On the 3rd of August, a month after the seizure of Donauwerth, and the invasion of Bavaria, the French Marshal Tallard, having made his way through the Black Forest with twenty-five thousand men, was able to reinforce the Elector at Augsburg. At the same time, Prince Eugene with eighteen thousand men reached Hochstadt on the Danube, a few miles above Donauwerth, and a week later he was joined by Marlborough. After an anxious consultation, and a careful reconnaissance, Marlborough and Eugene decided that on the 13th of August they would attack the French and Bavarians under Tallard and the Elector. The respective numbers of the opposing forces showed no very marked disparity, though the advantage was on the side of the French. But Eugene, to say nothing of Marlborough, was far superior in strategic capacity to any commander on the other side. The French, however, had more cannon than their opponents. They were encamped on the left bank of the Danube, at that point three hundred feet broad, and too deep for an army to cross. Tallard with his best infantry occupied the village of Blindheim on the same bank, henceforth known to Englishmen always as Blenheim, close to the spot where a little stream called the Nebel flows into the Danube. On the morning of the 13th of August, 1704, Marlborough with the greater part of the Allied Force confronted Tallard, while Eugene with a much smaller force was opposed to the Elector, and to Marsin. The Battle of Blenheim began at noon by a dashing charge upon the French which was led by Lord Cutts, "Salamander" Cutts, so named from his disregard of fire. But it was Marlborough himself who conducted the battle. He seemed to be everywhere. He commanded the cavalry in person, and it was a charge of cavalry which finally determined the fortune of the day. The fascination of his eager alacrity, and his intrepid calm, as he "taught the doubtful battle where to rage," breathed his own spirit into his men, and did far more than make up for the slight numerical inferiority of the Allies. At five in the afternoon a general charge, led by Marlborough himself, and at first repulsed, broke up the French troops, led by Tallard, and drove them into the Danube, where thousands of them were drowned. Tallard himself was taken prisoner. "M. Tallard and two other Generals are in my coach," wrote Marlborough to the Duchess, "and I am following the rest." At Blenheim itself, eleven thousand of the best troops in France were forced to an unconditional surrender, and this fact made an ineffaceable impression upon the Continent. On the 14th of August, Marlborough and Eugene entered Hochstadt together, joint champions of the liberties of Europe. They had fourteen thousand prisoners, of whom three thousand took service with the Allies. Of sixty thousand Frenchmen who went into the battle, not more than forty thousand came out from it free and unscathed. The losses of the Allies were comparatively small, and Eugene's force suffered far more severely than Marlborough's. Among those who distinguished themselves on the losing side a conspicuous place was won by the Irish Brigade, who fought against the country they detested, for the religion they loved.

In the same year, and the same month, which Blenheim has immortalized, Sir George Rooke, assisted by the Prince of Hesse-Darmstadt, captured Gibraltar from Philip of Spain. Human beings are not prophets, and little was thought of this conquest at the time. Its peculiar importance is due to Rooke. The German Prince, who accompanied him, was for hoisting the imperial flag. But Rooke, as an English Admiral, objected to so misleading a performance. England was the mistress of the seas; England had taken the Spanish fortress which commands entrance to the Mediterranean, and he promptly raised the English flag over the Rock, where it has ever since remained.

The seizure of Gibraltar was probably within the vast designs of Marlborough, whose plans were as wide as they were deep. But, for the moment, the stupendous victory of Blenheim diverted attention from Spain and the Mediterranean. The Queen was seated with the Duchess in the turret-chamber of Elizabeth's library at Windsor, when the famous note was brought to them, which Marlborough had scribbled from the field of battle in pencil to his wife. Below her lay the Thames, and the village of Eton, and the chapel of Henry the Sixth, and the tableland of Buckinghamshire, rolling up to the hills of Dropmore. Although modern trees, and still more modern buildings, have changed the face of the landscape, to imagine it as it was is not difficult, and on the wall there hangs a facsimile of the letter, surmounted by a portrait of the officer who conveyed the news. Mrs. Morley and Mrs. Freeman had already been drawn together by the ties of a common affliction, for the Duchess's only son. Lord Blandford, had died at Cambridge in 1703, three years after the Duke of Gloucester. They were now united in a common triumph, which was also a triumph for the nation, and for the liberties of Europe. Had it not been for Blenheim, and for Marlborough, the beautiful English country upon which the Queen looked that day might have been restored to Catholic domination, might even have become a province of France.

Louis the Fourteenth never quite recovered from the effects of Blenheim. Marlborough did what William of Orange tried to do against superior generals to Tallard and Marsin. He humbled to the dust the pride of France. He raised to a higher pitch than had ever been known before the martial glory of England. Strange character that he was, and full of mystery, he spent the night before Blenheim in prayer, and in receiving the sacrament with the rites of the English Church. Yet no one trusted him, and he did not deserve to be trusted. Men are the creatures of their age, and breathe fashionable views with the air in which they live. Marlborough's faults were, in kind, if not in degree, too common to be shocking. But they account for what has been too hastily stigmatized as the ingratitude of the English people towards him. Even on the morrow of Blenheim, when popular rejoicing at home was apparently universal and enthusiastic, the voice of the grumbler was heard. At that period Marlborough, whose political principles were vague and indefinite, was classed with the Whigs. It was a Whig war, and the Tories attacked it. What, they asked, was the use of killing Frenchmen? The French King could well spare as many more. What was the Holy Roman Empire to us that we should fight for it? An echo of such questions may be heard in Southey's poem about old Kaspar, sitting at his cottage door. The Empire, which Marlborough saved from premature extinction, was useful as a counterpoise to France, and French supremacy in Europe would have reduced England to the level she had reached in John Churchill's youth, when Charles the Second was King. It is for that very reason that the Jacobites attacked Marlborough, and depreciated Blenheim. On the other hand, it was Godolphin's fortune to procure through Charles Montagu, Earl of Halifax, a young Whig of singular promise, Joseph Addison of Magdalen College, Oxford, to celebrate the battle, and glorify the hero, in a poem, not a very good poem, called The Campaign. When Marlborough returned to London in December, he received the thanks of Parliament for his splendid achievements, and a more substantial reward in the Royal Manor of Woodstock, cleared of encumbrances by a vote of the Commons. In Woodstock Park the Queen built for him a palace to which she gave the name of Blenheim, a worthy monument of the taste that admired the architecture of Vanbrugh. Marlborough's victories improved the prospects of the party with which he was nominally connected, and at the General Election of 1705, required by the Triennial Act, the Whigs obtained a considerable majority. Marlborough and Godolphin were the real Government of the Queen. Their colleagues were ciphers.

In 1705 the party system was in process of crystallization, and had not assumed a definite shape. Whigs and Tories sat on opposite sides in both Houses of Parliament, but often sat together in the same Cabinet. Godolphin passed for a Tory. In 1704 he had taken into his government Robert Harley, a Tory of the moderate type, who actually became Secretary of State without at once ceasing to be Speaker, and Henry St. John as Secretary at War. Yet before the dissolution he made overtures to the Whig Junto, of whom Somers was the most eminent, and afterwards he gave the Great Seal to William Cowper, a Whig of the purest water. In this year, 1705, Harley surrendered the Speakership, remaining Secretary of State for the Northern Department, which included foreign affairs. Harley had the singular fortune to be intimately connected with men of genius, who made his name immortal. He had no shining talents, and his character, though for the age respectable, was of the ordinary kind. Yet Pope has devoted to him some of the noblest lines in the language, and the Journal to Stella proves that Swift was as fond of him as he could be of any man. He was indeed the Maecenas of his age, a genuine lover of literature, an assiduous collector of manuscripts, and a munificent patron of letters. He was also a sound administrator, without the financial capacity of

Godolphin, but well versed in the practice of Parliament and of the public offices, an unrivalled authority on the business and procedure of the House of Commons. He had been brought up in a Whig family, and in the principles of the Revolution, so that he was never able to share, though he sometimes found it convenient to simulate, the zeal against Nonconformists which animated the Tories of his time. What really united him with them, and made him their occasional leader, was his dislike of European intervention, his distrust of William's anti-Gallican policy, his denial that it was England's duty to maintain the balance of power, and his belief in peace at almost any price. It was the war, and the war alone, which separated him from the Whigs; and, though he held office when Marlborough won the battle of Blenheim, few Englishmen can have rejoiced in the victory less than he did. Harley loved wine, and shared the convivial habits of Queen Anne's reign. But, like Swift, he valued his bill of company more than his bill of fare, and he addicted himself to the society of his intellectual superiors without a particle of jealousy or of ostentation. Harley's colleague St. John was an almost complete antithesis to him. A born scholar, orator, and man of letters, the master of a brilliant and powerful, if somewhat too artificial style, St. John dazzled and charmed his readers and his hearers into thinking him a statesman of importance and weight. Although his oratory has wholly perished, the enthusiastic admiration of his contemporaries must be accepted as conclusive testimony to its merits. His writings, though Burke declared that no man then read them, and that no man had ever read them through, have been extolled by many later critics, for instance Matthew Arnold and Lord Stanhope, as models of lucid and idiomatic English. But he added nothing in his long life to the strength, the welfare, or the prosperity of his country, because his character had no foundation. A free thinker and a loose liver, he was a Jacobite in the service of a Parliamentary Sovereign, and he would if he could, have substituted the personal rule of a popular monarch for the ordered freedom of the revolutionary settlement. The best of boon companions, he was the most unprincipled of politicians, and, in the opinion of his own father, the chief question raised at the outset of his career was, whether he would be hanged or beheaded.

Few contrasts in history are more striking than the association of Queen Anne with the scholars and statesmen of her court and cabinet. A narrowminded and illiterate woman, devoted to her favourite Duchess, who had no more learning than herself, and in a feminine way to the pleasures of the table, she never seemed to realize the fact that her reign was made illustrious by the verse of Pope, and the prose of Swift, as well as by the finance of Godolphin, and the arms of Marlborough. She visited in due course the ancient Universities, and in April 1705, she had the honour of knighting Isaac Newton at Cambridge. But the last of the Stuarts differed from the last of the Tudors, and from the rest of her own race, in no respect more strongly than in her blank indifference to the things of the mind. Anne was not without taste for pleasure, or enjoyment of life. Although she did not care for literature, she loved music, and was so fond of driving, and of sport, that Swift, when he came to Windsor, called her a Jehu and a Nimrod. It was her vanity to think that she ruled as well as reigned. But no public act made her so popular as her revival of the superstitious practice, discontinued by William, and known as "touching for the King's evil." The King's evil was scrofula, and one of the children whom she fruitlessly touched was Samuel Johnson.

On the last day of March 1705 Marlborough left England, sailing from Harwich for the Hague. His main object was a renewal of military operations, then always suspended from the autumn to the spring. But so much hampered was he by the reluctance of the States General, and so much irritated by the Tory attacks upon him at home, that he wrote to Godolphin in June expressing weariness of his life. The Empire was no better than the Republic. The death of the Emperor Leopold in May, and the succession of the Emperor Joseph, King of the Romans, produced no improvement. Prince Eugene, upon whom alone Marlborough could rely, was sent to Italy, and with Prince Louis of Baden he could do nothing at all. While he was chafing and fuming with an impatience he rarely displayed, a glittering adventurer, who does not deserve to be named in connection with him, achieved in Spain the one real success of his life. Charles Mordaunt, third Earl of Peterborough, had been despatched by Marlborough himself to the Peninsula with an auxiliary force, Dutch and English, of seven thousand men. Sir Cloudesley Shovel joined him at Gibraltar as Admiral of the Fleet. Before reaching Gibraltar, however, Peterborough took up the Archduke Charles, the candidate of the Allies for the throne of Spain, who had not yet been able to set foot in the dominions he claimed. They landed in Valencia, where Charles was received with enthusiasm, and Peterborough proposed an immediate advance upon Madrid. In this, however, he was overruled by a council of war, and the expedition next sailed to Barcelona. A long and wearisome siege followed.

By the middle of September 1705, the failure of the enterprise seemed so certain, that the inhabitants of the town celebrated by public rejoicings the inevitable departure of the heretics. At this moment the desultory mind of Peterborough hit for once upon a practical expedient. On the side of Barcelona which is away from the sea rises the hill of Montjuich, with a castle and a garrison at the top. The garrison, believing their position to be impregnable, expected no attack. For that very reason Peterborough led a small force up the hill at midnight, surprised the Spanish troops, scaled the heights, and took the citadel. General Stanhope, following with a reserve, supported his chief, and the vantage-ground was secured. Within a month Barcelona had fallen, and Charles had at least secured a footing in the kingdom of Spain. Peterborough became a popular hero. Swift wrote

"Mordanto fills the trump of fame,
The Christian worlds his deeds proclaim,
And prints are crowded with his name."

His daredevil recklessness, and the profusion with which he squandered any money he had, compared favourably with the rapacious meanness of Marlborough. It is related of him that he was once mistaken for the Duke, and mobbed as he came from the House of Lords. "Gentlemen," said he, "I will give you two proofs that I am not the Duke of Marlborough. In the first place I have only five guineas in my pocket. In the second place they are very much at your service." Yet Peterborough scarcely belongs to history. He had no principles, no character, no fixed resolutions of any kind. He was in truth more than half mad, and he flashes but for an instant across the world's horizon. It will not be necessary to mention him any more.

The sleepless genius of Marlborough, unhasting, unresting, had devised for the year 1706 a new plan of campaign. He would march with an allied force on Italy, and join Prince Eugene. So earnest, however, were the remonstrances of the Dutch, who feared a French invasion if he left them, that he changed his plans, and entered Flanders in May. On the 23rd of the month, he and General Cadogan, almost his only real friend, with about sixty thousand men, English and Dutch, met Marshal Villeroy, with rather superior numbers, at the village of Ramillies on the Little Gheet. There was fought the second of Marlborough's great victories, equally decisive with Blenheim, though much less sanguinary and protracted. Marlborough was associated with the Dutch Marshal Overkirk, and Villeroy with the luckless Maximilian, Elector of Bavaria. The French and Bavarians lost fifteen thousand men, the Allies not above a fourth part of that number. Brussels was evacuated by the French troops, and Marlborough entered it in triumph. Ghent, Bruges, and Oudenarde likewise surrendered. The French garrison of Antwerp marched out with the honours of war.

At Ramillies Marlborough had the narrowest escape of his life. He was surrounded by a party of French dragoons, who recognized him, and tried to take him prisoner. He rode at a ditch, but his horse refused the leap, and threw him. While he was mounting another horse, as his equerry held his stirrup, a cannon-ball carried off the equerry's head. He himself escaped with severe bruises, and led in person the final charge on Ramillies.

A public thanksgiving for this victory was appointed to be held in England on the 27th of June, and, at least in public, all was elation there. In France things were naturally different. Nobody made any attempt on this occasion to conceal the extent and magnitude of the disaster. Although Marlborough, with reluctant prudence, declined the lucrative and splendid offer that he should be Lieutenant-Governor of the Netherlands for the Archduke Charles, now styled Charles the Third of Spain, he was in reality Dictator of Europe. His very name set up a panic, and there was scarcely a Marshal of France who would have cared to meet him in the field after the experience of Tallard and Villeroy. Louis the pseudo-great had no true courage. He was abjectly superstitious, and a craven at heart. Although he treated his unsuccessful generals with French and kingly courtesy, he recognized that the game was up. He was willing, and let it be known that he was willing, to acknowledge Charles as lawful King of Spain, and Anne as lawful Queen of England, if Naples, Sicily, and Milan were ceded to his grandson, Philip of Anjou. With this offer Marlborough and the English Government might well have closed. If it did not give England all that she wanted, it was an outward and visible sign that France no longer dominated Europe. It amounted to a formal confession of defeat from the haughtiest despot that had ever threatened the independence of this country. But Marlborough's ambition was insatiable, and his trade was war. He used his unrivalled influence, the influence of a man who has conquered apparently invincible foes, to such purpose, both with Godolphin in London, and with Pensionary Heinsius at the Hague, that he was authorized to continue the campaign. The Dutch were bound to him by the strongest ties of gratitude. He had the ear of his own Sovereign, not because he was the greatest commander since Julius Caesar, but because he was the husband of Sarah Jennings. When he returned home at the end of

1706, equally triumphant in counsel and in war, his Dukedom was entailed upon his daughters and their sons, his own son, the Marquess of Blandford, having died in early manhood; and his son-in-law, the Earl of Sunderland, founder of the splendid library at Althorp, was made a Secretary of State.

In 1706 was prepared, and in 1707 was consummated, the Union between England and Scotland. Since the accession of James the First, which introduced the Stuarts to England, the two countries had been united, except during the Commonwealth, by the golden link of the Crown alone. Want of a closer tie, which Cromwell had temporarily formed, led to much inconvenience, especially in matters of trade, which required custom-houses on the frontier for its regulation, and provoked smuggling, as the protective duties then universal always do. The Scottish people, moreover, were demanding the same commercial privileges as England enjoyed, abroad as well as at home, and one risk in refusing the demand was that Scotland might form an alliance with France. The policy of a Parliamentary union was not new. Although Cromwell's Union was dissolved at the Restoration, William made several attempts to restore it, and Anne herself, as we know, and other authorities, from Clerk of Penicuik, had it much at heart. Defoe, who spent a great deal of time at Edinburgh, kept Harley constantly informed of Scottish opinion, and impressed upon him that the alternative was union or war. It must be remembered that England was at war already. If peace had been made after Ramillies, the Treaty of Union would have been less urgent, though equally essential. But the Government had yielded to Marlborough's opinion that the struggle for Continental supremacy should go on. If Scotland had taken the side of France, the difficulties would have been multiplied, and the result uncertain. Ireland was already hostile, being predominantly Catholic, and mainly disaffected. To make the interests of England the interests of Scotland too was the part of wise and prudent statesmanship, of just and considerate foresight. Anne's genuine zeal for the union was, from a personal point of view, the most creditable incident of her reign, as it was politically the most lasting and successful. Before William died the commercial situation had become almost intolerable. The woollen manufactures of England had been excluded from the northern kingdom, in revenge for the King's refusal to help the Scottish colonists of Darien, dupes of William Paterson's madcap scheme, and of their own insane credulity, against the Spanish troops who expelled them. On the 16th of April, 1706, English and Scottish Commissioners met in the

Cockpit at Whitehall. There were sixty-two of them, thirty-one upon each side, whose signatures may be read in the Scottish copy of the Treaty kept at Windsor, where Anne is described as Queen of Scotland, England, France, and Ireland. But a single man took the lead, and kept it. Lord Somers was head and shoulders above his colleagues. He saw that if equal privileges of commerce between London and Edinburgh were the chief inducement which Scotland had for engaging in the Treaty of Union, English interests were principally concerned in preventing the use of the northern kingdom, especially the Highlands, as a nucleus of Jacobite plots. Very few days sufficed for setting the preliminary propositions to be laid before Parliament in due course. Lord Chancellor Cowper formally moved, and Lord Seafield, Chancellor of Scotland, seconded, that the two countries should be united in one kingdom, called Great Britain; that there should be one British Parliament, and one only; and that the succession to the British, not merely the English, Crown should be regulated by the Act of Settlement. A single system of taxation, the natural consequence of political union, increased the amount hitherto paid by the Scottish people; but by way of set off, a grant of four hundred thousand pounds, known as the Equivalent, was made to Scotland from the English exchequer for the encouragement of manufactures, and in partial compensation for the loss of Darien. When this financial detail had been arranged, the rest of the business went smoothly enough. The separate Chancellorship of Scotland was abolished, and one Great Seal for both countries was ordered to be struck. But the Lord Chancellor acquired no legal jurisdiction in Scotland, except as a Peer of Parliament when appeals came to the House of Lords. The Court of Session remained intact, and continued to administer the Scottish system of law, founded on the Roman, totally different from the English. That the Episcopal Church of England, and the Presbyterian Church of Scotland, should be alone recognized by the State was taken as a fundamental article, which the Commissioners were precluded by the terms of their appointment from even discussing. The Stuarts had had enough of trying to force episcopacy upon the Covenanters north of the Tweed. The number of Scottish members in the British House of Commons was fixed at forty-five, and the number of Scottish Representative Peers to sit in the House of Lords at sixteen. It was inferred from this provision that no Peers of Scotland were henceforth to be, nor have they since been, created. No Scottish Peer could sit, or has ever sat, in the British House of Commons. The House of Lords passed a Resolution which was observed, and not rescinded, till 1784, that no Peer of Scotland could be made a Peer of Great Britain. This Treaty was submitted first to the Scottish, and afterwards to the English, Parliament. In Scotland the union was opposed by the Jacobites, who judged quite correctly that it had been aimed as a blow at their cause, and by the High-flying Preachers, especially the Cameronians, who considered that to have anything in common with Prelatists was an abominable sin. In the city of Edinburgh the merchants apprehended some loss of custom from the removal of Parliament men to London, and throughout the country there were those whose national pride represented to them that union would mean absorption in England. Their feelings were fantastically, but vigorously, expressed by Lord Belhaven. The Ratification of the Union was not finally carried in Edinburgh till the 16th of January, 1707, after it had been determined that the representative Peers of Scotland should be chosen by the whole of the Scottish Peerage for the term of a single Parliament, then three years. "There," said Lord Seafield, in a picturesque and memorable phrase, "there is the end of an old song." At Westminster, the Act of Union passed with great rapidity, "post haste," as some indignant Tories exclaimed. But Harley and St. John controlled the moderate men, while the extreme Jacobites were not numerous enough to cause much delay. High Churchmen, inclined to protest against the formal recognition of Presbyterianism, were quieted with the assurance, such as it was, that an Episcopal Church of England was equally part of the Constitution. The injustice of forcing an alien Church upon the people of Ireland does not seem to have struck any one at that time, nor indeed would it have been possible to recognize the religion of the Pretender. Catholic emancipation, either in Great Britain or in Ireland, would have been difficult, if not impossible, while the Jacobites were strong and dangerous. On the 6th of March, 1707, Queen Anne gave her assent to the Act of Union, which came into operation upon the 1st of May, and thus the last of the Stuarts united the Legislatures, as the first of the Stuarts had united the Crowns.

Early in the year 1707 the hopes of the French King were revived by the bait of a profitable alliance. The young King of Sweden, Charles the Twelfth, had achieved by his successes in Poland, where he put down one sovereign and set up another, a military reputation second to Marlborough's alone. It all came to nothing, and Charles the Twelfth would have been justly forgotten long ago if two men of genius, as wide asunder as the poles, had not combined to give him a double immortality.

Voltaire's History is a standard book, Carlyle thought his best piece of writing, and Johnson's Vanity of Human Wishes embalms the man who "left a name at which the world grew pale, to point a moral and adorn a tale." It is a poor tale, and a cheap moral. Charles wasted his life, and exhausted his country, in futile campaigns against enemies of his own making, until a stray bullet put an end to his career. But at the beginning of 1707 he had forty thousand men in Saxony, and if he joined them to the army of France, who could still count upon Bavaria, the result to the empire might be disastrous. So grave did the situation seem that the services of Marlborough were invoked to deal with it, and to counteract the designs of Louis. Marlborough was a consummate diplomatist, and his serene, victorious intellect shone with equally unclouded radiance upon a battle or an intrigue. He could not entirely conceal his scorn of the vainglorious Swede, and his effusive compliments on the prowess of that barrack-room hero are insults imperfectly disguised. When he visited the Swedish camp at Alt Ranstadt, he said, perhaps without a visible sneer, "I wish I could serve some campaign under so great a general as your Majesty, that I might learn what I yet want to know in the art of war." Marlborough was an almost unerring judge of men, and he knew that his victim would swallow the flattery. Then he talked, and waited, and watched. On his way to Saxony from the Hague, he had called at Hanover, and consulted the Elector, whose mother was heir presumptive to the British throne. George characteristically recommended bribes, which Marlborough was not above giving at the public expense, and the Swedish Ministers were not above taking for themselves. But Marlborough would have succeeded without such aid. To a mind like his the task must have been child's play. He soon found, as Voltaire informs us, that Charles was jealous of Louis, and that a map of Russia lay open on his table. He suggested that an invasion of the Czar's dominions would receive aid from the Cossack Mazeppa, and would put Charles the Twelfth on a higher pinnacle of fame than Louis the Fourteenth. The trick was won. When Marlborough returned to the Hague on the 8th of May, having been absent from the Dutch capital less than three weeks, Charles had struck his camp, and disappeared from the purview of the Allies.

Nevertheless, when Marlborough returned to England in November 1707, having concluded the year's campaign with the approach of winter, he found the country dissatisfied and despondent. Since Ramillies there had been no military success worthy of the name, and the prospect of an honourable peace seemed remote. A great naval catastrophe saddened the autumn. On the 22nd of October Sir Cloudesley Shovel, who had risen from the position of a cabin-boy to be Admiral of the Fleet, went down among the Scilly Isles in his flagship Association with nine hundred men. There was no poet to rank the Association with the Royal George. But there was another Royal George, Prince George of Denmark, whose hopeless incompetence as Lord High Admiral had become more conspicuous than it otherwise would have been through the rapacity and inefficiency of Admiral Churchill, the great Duke's brother, his creature and tool. The Admiral's retention in office was a scandal, not the less odious because Churchill did, so far as it was done at all, the work which the Queen's husband received money for not doing. Meanwhile the influence of the Churchills at Court had begun to wane. It had been wielded by the Duchess only, and her Grace had abused her power. The Queen was a pious Churchwoman, and a Tory. The Duchess, so far as she had any politics, was a Whig, caring nothing for the Church, and very little for religion of any kind. Her sordid avarice, her scornful temper, and her ungovernable rage were driving Anne into sullen rebellion. A favourite the Queen must have. She wanted some one to lean upon, and her husband was nought. The proud Duchess looked with a contemptuous eye upon Abigail Hill, a poor relation of her own, for whom she had herself procured a place at Court as a woman of the bedchamber. Abigail was a very quiet, and a very artful girl. She had contrived to give herself a good education, which the Duchess was almost wholly without; her powers of mind were considerable, and she formed unobtrusively a close alliance with her kinsman, Secretary Harley. Her political opinions were his and the Queen's. She was an orthodox Churchwoman, and poor Anne found her placid temper a sure relief from the tempestuous reproaches of "Mrs. Freeman." Abigail Hill enters the sphere of history in 1707, the date of her secret marriage with Samuel Masham, a gentleman-in-waiting to Prince George. Discovery of this clandestine union, perfectly regular as it was, made the Duchess furious. But her violence against Mrs. Masham only widened her breach with the Queen, and established the new favourite's position.

The first Parliament of Great Britain, which met on the 23rd of October, 1707, passed through both Houses joint resolutions in favour of continuing the war so long as Spain, or any part of the Spanish monarchy, remained under the House of Bourbon. This was the Whig policy, the policy put forward by Lord Somers, ablest survivor of the statesmen who had made the Revolution, and had placed William of Orange on the British throne. Its avowal at this juncture made Marlborough a Whig, not perhaps with the less willingness on his part because his unpopular bother at the Admiralty was a violent and irrepressible Tory. Before Parliament met in 1708 Godolphin, acting in concert with Whigs outside the Cabinet, and especially with Marlborough, determined that Harley must go. The struggle was long and obstinate. The Queen, supported by Mrs. Masham, clung to her favourite Minister, not so much because he was a Tory, as because he was, or professed to be, a High Churchman. Somers, more powerful at that moment than any Minister, carried a measure for cementing the union with Scotland by the abolition of the separate Privy Council which North Britain had hitherto possessed. On this point, and on others, the Cabinet was at sixes and sevens. The Queen habitually attended the confidential meetings of her servants, which it was then the fashion to hold on Sundays. On Sunday, the 8th of February, 1708, the Cabinet met at Kensington in the absence of Godolphin, Lord Treasurer, and Marlborough, Captain General. The two Prime Ministers, whose authority was really equal, refused to attend so long as Harley remained a servant of the Crown. The Queen would gladly have accepted Godolphin's resignation, and might possibly have been induced to accept Marlborough's. But Harley saw that he was beaten, or perhaps that the sooner he went, the sooner he would come back on his own terms. Three days afterwards he resigned, along with St. John, and the Cabinet became, in the rapidly shifting nomenclature of that time, exclusively Whig. As usual, the most significant part of the transaction was that which attracted least notice at the time. Henry St. John's successor at the War Office was a young Norfolk squire named Robert Walpole.

The victory of the Whigs, to give them the name which they gave themselves, was for the moment complete. Godolphin and Marlborough used and abused their triumph. They insisted that the Queen, w-ho had been making ecclesiastical appointments on her own account from the ranks of Tories and High Churchmen, should for the future be guided by the advice of her Whig Ministers in the Church as well as in the State. They could not deny that Anne had chosen pious and excellent men. Where religion or morality was concerned, she was always strictly conscientious. But, with motives which were certainly not of the highest, the Lord Treasurer and the Captain General were asserting a principle which has ever since prevailed, and is essential to the maintenance of the Constitution. The Crown cannot be responsible to Parliament, except in case of revolution or civil war. For every act of the Sovereign some Minister must be prepared to answer in the House of Commons, and he cannot be expected to defend a course or a policy of which he disapproves. The Church of England being established by law, being in fact part of the Constitution, Parliament has a right to know the reason why a particular clergyman is made a Bishop, or a Dean, or a Regius Professor of Divinity. Anne sullenly acquiesced in what she regarded as the tyranny of her Ministers, and privately sought occasion to overthrow them. She had, however, some time to wait, relying upon Harley's friend, the faithful Abigail. Harley himself was accused of high treason in the common form of those days, correspondence with St. Germains. The charge, which may have been premature, broke down for want of positive evidence, and Harley was not formally impeached. He was left in an atmosphere of suspicion which rendered him an object of hatred and distrust among Protestants, Low Churchmen, and Whigs.

The General Election of 1708 gave the Whig Ministry a preponderance in the House of Commons, and there was a steady Whig majority in the House of Lords. It was no mere question of party nicknames. The friends of "James the Third," a dull youth, but an ardent Catholic, were active and venturesome. They planned an invasion of Scotland, where the large party who had opposed the Union were favourable to their cause, and Madame de Maintenon, who was Queen, if not King, of France, in everything but name, lent all her influence to support the Pretender. This expedition failed ingloriously. But the Queen's throne was not secure from what she called, or was made to call, "the designs of a Popish Pretender, bred up in the principles of the most arbitrary government." The Whig Ministry, which was really the Ministry of Marlborough, determined to prosecute the war, and early in April 1708 the ever-victorious Captain left England for Holland, that he might consult Prince Eugene and Pensionary Heinsius at the Hague. At this consultation it was decided to fight the French in the Netherlands, and Marlborough made Brussels his headquarters, while Eugene, after an interview with the Emperor at Vienna, took up a position on the Moselle. The situation in the Netherlands was unfavourable to the Allies. The States had made themselves so unpopular in Brabant that the chief cities, Ghent and Bruges, surrendered almost without resistance to the French. This was on the 5th of July, and then Marlborough, with his unerring vision, perceived that he must strike the enemy at once. On the 9th the French army began the siege of Oudenarde on the river Schelde. Sending General Cadogan, a renowned soldier, to occupy Lessines, which the French had designed for cover, Marlborough moved quickly upon the Schelde opposite Oudenarde on the morning of the nth. His force was in numbers inferior to the French. But it was directed by the genius of a single commander, while the army of Louis suffered from the nominal supremacy of the Duke of Burgundy, a Prince of the blood, over the Duke of Vendome, a scandalous ruffian and debauchee, but a gallant and skilful commander. Marlborough was loyally assisted by Eugene, who never failed to acknowledge the surpassing talents of a man he was great enough loyally to serve. The battle began at three in the afternoon, and lasted until the long summer day had faded into darkness. The French right was cut off, under Marlborough's directions, by Marshal Overkirk, with twenty battalions of Dutch and Danes. The shades of evening fell upon the entire defeat of Vendome, who retreated unwillingly towards Ghent, leaving thousands of prisoners in the hands of the Allies. "We have taken," wrote Marlborough to Godolphin, "ninety-five colours and standards, besides three the Prussians keep to send to their King," the Elector of Brandenburg, who had just been crowned King of Prussia. After the battle of Oudenarde Marlborough would have marched into the heart of France, and so put an end to the war. But this splendid design was too audacious even for Prince Eugene, and much more so for the Dutch deputies of the States. The capture of Lille, in itself daring enough, was the utmost length to which Marlborough could carry the Allies. It was a formidable task. Lille had been fortified by Vauban, the first military engineer of that age. Marshal Boufflers, the Governor, had a garrison of fifteen thousand men. The French were in possession of Ghent, which commanded the course of the Schelde. Nevertheless, Eugene, covered by Marlborough, began the siege on the 22nd of August, 1708, and just two months later Boufflers surrendered. This brilliant achievement was made possible by the battle of Wynendale, where, on the 28th of September, General Webb repulsed the French attack from Bruges under La Mothe, designed to cut off a convoy of supplies from Ostend for the relief of the besiegers. Before the end of the year Marlborough had recovered from the French both Ghent and Bruges. To the haughty monarch who had revoked the Edict of Nantes he must have seemed like the scourge of God.

When the Parliament of 1708 met on the 16th of November, the power of the Whigs seemed to be established, and their ascendency was for the time complete. On the 28th of October Prince George of Denmark, natus consumere fruges, had drunk his last bottle, and departed this life, having perhaps done as little good, and as little harm, as it is possible for a human being in a high position to do. His creature Admiral Churchill was at once dismissed from the Admiralty, the Admiral's illustrious brother being entirely indifferent to his fate, and Lord Pembroke became head of the Board. Pembroke's place as President of the Council was taken by John, Lord Somers, the most justly famous of those great lawyers who have maintained the liberties of England in troubled and dangerous times. To Somers is mainly due the Declaration of Rights, and he had taken a leading part in the Treaty of Union with Scotland. His influence in the House of Lords was almost unbounded, and an attempt to impeach him in the last days of King William had ignominiously failed. His public character was stainless, and his enemies were so destitute of material for calumny that they were driven to accuse him of undue susceptibility to the charms of the other sex. But he was identified with the Revolution, and therefore obnoxious to Queen Anne, a Jacobite Sovereign with a Parliamentary title. Godolphin, aided by Marlborough, extorted from her with great difficulty her consent to declare Somers Lord President of the Council, and Wharton Lord Lieutenant of Ireland. Her Majesty's objections to Lord Wharton were neither unnatural nor discreditable. He was a coarse profligate and blasphemer, utterly without principle both in public and private life, pronounced by Swift, not often random in his abuse, to be the most universal villain he had ever known. But Wharton was always a staunch Whig, and in the triumph of the Whig party he could not be neglected. The Queen was made to feel in the hour of her bereavement that she was the puppet of a faction, and the iron entered into her soul. Her miseries were not alleviated by the joint Address from both Houses in January 1709, praying her to contract for the public interest a second marriage. If we consider what Anne's maternal experience had been, and that she was now forty-five years old, this request must appear not only discourteous, but repugnant to decency and humanity. The Queen declined to give a "particular answer," and consoled herself with the company of Mrs. Masham. She refused to see any member of the House of Hanover, and would not listen to the suggestion that the Electress Sophia, heir presumptive to the throne, or her son the Elector, or her grandson the

Electoral Prince, Duke of Cambridge in the English peerage, who had fought gallantly for the allies at Oudenarde, should be invited to England. The prospects of the succession might well make British statesmen uneasy. It was now practically certain that Anne would not have issue, and no man could say for certain who would succeed her. The Act of Settlement was clear enough, for it fixed the Crown in the Protestant branch of James the First's descendants. But an Act of Parliament can always be repealed, and if a Tory House of Commons were elected in three years, or in six, the Chevalier de St. George, as the French called him, might be adopted, in case he gave up his Popish religion, as James the Third. The Queen's predecessor had been a Dutchman. Her successor would be a German. The Catholic Highlands of Scotland were ready to rise for the Pretender. How many Tories were also Jacobites no human being could precisely tell. Although some men of education and intelligence still firmly believed in the story of the warming-pan, which made James Stuart a supposititious child, there was not a particle of evidence to prove it, it had indeed been disproved, and it was gradually falling into disrepute. The Queen's deep and sincere affection for the Protestant Church of England, the only strong element in her character, and the guiding principle of her life, prevented her from acknowledging her brother to have a higher title than her own. James himself, a man of sense and courage, though not attractive or interesting, had fought with the French at Oudenarde, and it was notorious that there were English Jacobites who, like Fielding's Squire Western, fervently desired the success of the French arms. Among public men there was general and mutual distrust, for no one knew who might be corresponding with the Pretender, or on what terms. It is practically certain that if James would have abandoned the Roman Catholic faith, he might have been King of England on his sister's death, and there was no guarantee that his Catholicism would bear a strain which had broken down the nominal Protestantism of Henry the Fourth. If Paris was worth a mass, London might be worth a Bible. The Whigs were considered at Court to be not only hard taskmasters, but much tainted with irreligion, and Marlborough's attachment to the principles of the Reformation, though the one genuine feeling in his nature, except his love for Sarah, had certainly not much influence upon his public conduct. But, treacherous as he was, he was true to Protestantism, and the War of the Succession in Spain was also a; war for the Protestant Succession in England.

Of that war Louis the Fourteenth had had more than enough. His long reign, the longest in European history, was closing in ruin and disgrace. The massacre and expulsion of the Huguenots in 1685 had deprived France of her ablest and most industrious manufacturers and artisans. William of Orange, though his campaign in the Netherlands was indecisive, and partook largely of defence, had baffled the plans and drained the resources of the French King. Marlborough had completed what William began, and France was perishing for lack of manhood. The miserable superstition of the doting monarch and his pious spouse sought rather to expiate by penance the sins of his youth than to repair by prudence the errors of his manhood. An atmosphere of devotion was prescribed at Versailles, and, as Macaulay dryly puts it, the Marshals of France were much in prayer. But their prayers, as might in the circumstances have been expected, availed them nothing, and after Oudenarde, as after Ramillies, the King sued humbly for peace. De Torcy, his Minister for Foreign Affairs, made overtures to Heinsius, the head of the Government at the Hague. His object was to detach Holland from Great Britain, and conclude a separate treaty with the Dutch States. But Heinsius was a friend of Marlborough, and thoroughly loyal to the Alliance. He declined to treat alone, and he indicated, moreover, in quite uncompromising language, the preliminary concessions which France would have to make. The Empire must be secured in possession of Spain and the Spanish Indies, of Naples and Sicily, and of the Netherlands. As for the Dutch themselves, they must have a barrier of strong towns to protect them against the possibility of invasion. This, however, was not enough for the British Government. Marlborough, who returned from the Hague to London in March 1709, urged upon his colleagues demands still more irksome, to which he obtained their consent. Louis must acknowledge the Protestant Succession in Great Britain, expel the Pretender from France, and demolish the fortifications of Dunkirk, from which the invading squadron had sailed for Scotland. Both the Houses of Parliament agreed to the proposals of the Cabinet, and with these instructions, really drawn by himself, Marlborough, accompanied by Lord Townshend as second Plenipotentiary, met Prince Eugene from Vienna at the Dutch capital in April. The first French Plenipotentiary was President Rouille. But in his extreme desire for peace de Torcy came himself and on the 27th of May received from Heinsius the requisitions of the Allies. Newfoundland was claimed for England. Ten fortresses in Flanders must be assigned to the Dutch as a barrier. When these points, and those previously put forward, had been accepted by France, the consideration given her would not be a lasting peace, but simply and solely a truce for two months from the 1st of June to the 1st of August. During that time the Duke of Anjou, pretending to be King of Spain, and being actually in possession of Castille, which he held without French aid, was to leave the Peninsula, and take up his abode in France. If he failed to do so of his own accord, the King of France, his own grandfather, was to join the Allies in compelling him. De Torcy at once declared that he had no authority to make any such engagement, and the negotiations were broken off. It is impossible to justify the policy of the Whig Government in refusing the honourable peace which they might have obtained, and insisting upon terms so humiliating that a high-spirited people like the French were driven to reject them. Even Marlborough thought them too hard, and withheld his name from the Barrier Treaty, signed by Townshend, which gave the Dutch a guarantee for their ten fortresses at the close of the war. On the 2nd of June Louis held a council, attended by de Torcy, at Versailles. The demands of the Allies were formally rejected, and the war was renewed.

Marlborough and Eugene took joint command of the allied army in Flanders, estimated to consist of a hundred and ten thousand men. Marshal Villars, who opposed them, had an inferior force, ill armed, ill clothed, and ill fed. When Godolphin was at the Treasury, and Marlborough in the field, British soldiers never suffered from want of raiment, ammunition, or supplies. Instead of attacking Villars on the plains of Sens, the allied commanders invested Tournay on the 7th of July, and took it in three weeks. Mons, the capital of Hainault, was next besieged, and Villars, who had been joined by Boufflers, the defender of Lille, marched to its relief. On the nth of September, about seven in the morning, Marlborough and Eugene fell upon him at the village of Malplaquet, and a most sanguinary encounter followed. The numbers were nearly equal, about a hundred thousand on each side, and the French fought with desperate courage. Marlborough exposed his life as freely as if he had been a young subaltern in his first engagement, and the slaughter was terrible. The battle lasted seven hours, and at the end of it the French were driven from their position. But they retreated in good order, and the losses of the Allies were far greater than their own. "We have had this day," wrote Marlborough to his wife, "a very bloody battle; the first part of the day we beat their foot and afterwards their horse." Even Marlborough was moved to real concern by the sight of Malplaquet after the engagement, and he must have felt that the lives lost were thrown away. For there were no reasonable conditions which Louis would not, through de Torcy, have accepted in the spring of 1709. The immediate and the sole result of Malplaquet was the surrender of Mons, which capitulated on the 20th of October.

At this moment Marlborough, flushed with victory, and stimulated by his Duchess, made the one fatal mistake of his glorious, infamous career. He held the office of Captain General, or Commander-in-Chief, during the pleasure of the Crown. He requested the Queen to confer it upon him by Letters Patent for the term of his natural life. From the military point of view the proposal was not altogether unreasonable. Marlborough's genius for war is without a parallel in the history of the modern world. Compared with him Napoleon was reckless of life, and Wellington devoid of originality. Caesar's thrasonical boast might have been made in sober earnest by John Churchill. When he had come, and seen, he had already conquered. The Marshals of France were his washpot. Over Louis the Fourteenth he had cast his shoe. He never besieged a town without taking it, or fought a battle without winning it. A still greater fame is his. Given the object which he desired to achieve, he never wasted lives in achieving it. Even at Malplaquet, bloody as it was, there had been no useless or avoidable slaughter on the side of the Allies. Nor was he less triumphant in negotiation than in war. His infallible tact and his irresistible charm made statesmen and potentates the instruments of his sovereign will, so long as the power of France was dangerous to the peace of Europe, and the Protestant succession to the throne of Great Britain was insecure. But his success had been so complete that he had ceased to be indispensable, and the peril of his own inordinate cupidity seemed far more imminent to the British Constitution than the designs of the Pretender at St. Germains, or of the decrepit, exploded impostor at Versailles. Even the Whig Chancellor, Cowper, rejected as unconstitutional the claims of the Whig General to be recompensed by a novel Dictatorship for a Whig war. The Queen herself was not much concerned with the arguments which prevailed upon lawyers like Cowper; but she had been for some time surely, though gradually, transferring her affections from the Duchess of Marlborough, who worried her with reproaches, to Mrs. Masham, who soothed her with compliments. There was only one person who could endure the Duchess's temper, and that was the Duke. His patience in bearing her stormy outbursts was not the least wonderful part of his unruffled affability and calm. He had been gifted by nature, and had cultivated by assiduous art an easy, happy, placable disposition, which gave enjoyment to every one who came near him, and not least to himself. He charmed every one without caring for any one, and was agreeable because he liked it. The Duchess, except in her love of money, was nothing that he was, and everything that he was not. She had made herself intolerable at Court, as she would have made herself intolerable anywhere. Mrs. Masham, whose intelligence was far above the common, did not fail to take advantage of Sarah's blunders, and the Duke's petition was rejected. The Whigs did not know how to manage the Queen, who had inherited her father's sullen and obstinate temper. For the moment, however, they were successful. They required that she should dismiss Lord Pembroke from the Admiralty, and appoint in his room Edward Russell, Earl of Orford, who had been ennobled by William the Third for his naval victory over the French at Barfleur in 1692, but was generally believed to have been connected with the intrigues of Marlborough's nephew, Berwick. With Orford's appointment the power of the Whigs reached its zenith, Marlborough returned from the wars on the 8th of November, 1709. Parliament met on the 15th, and the House of Commons voted a sum of six millions sterling, without hesitation, for the continuance of the campaign.

CHAPTER II: POLITICS — II

When the Whigs were at the height of their power, an unforeseen, and, to a superficial observer, a trifling incident, produced a convulsion, and led to a catastrophe. The numerous and powerful body of political High Churchmen, among whom Francis Atterbury, then Dean of Carlisle, was the most eminent and intrepid, raised a cry that the Church was in danger. By the union with Presbyterian Scotland Presbyterians had been necessarily admitted to both Houses of Parliament, from which Catholics were excluded by the Test Act. The occasional conformity of those Dissenters who took the sacrament in the Church of England as a qualification for municipal office gave great offence to jealous ecclesiastics, and several attempts had been made without success to prevent this mode of escape from the statute. The Form of Prayer for the thirtieth of January stamped with official approval a strange and blasphemous comparison between the execution of Charles the First and the Passion of Christ. Atterbury, who was a Jacobite, and many other clergymen, though they would not acknowledge the Pope, were much nearer to the Church of Rome than to Protestant Dissent, and pushed the doctrine of divine right, with its corollary of passive obedience, far beyond the point where it would have been logically consistent with allegiance to Queen Anne. They abhorred the principles of 1688, and regarded the Revolution much as their modern successors regard the Reformation. A turbulent specimen of this class, Henry Sacheverell, Doctor of Divinity and Fellow of Magdalen College, Oxford, had been elected by popular votes, a rare anomaly in the Church of England, to the benefice of St. Saviour's, Southwark. There he preached his favourite doctrines with much animation, and engaged in vehement controversy with Benjamin Hoadly, a Low Churchman and a Whig, who was at that time Rector of St. Peter le Poer in the City of London. In August 1709, Sacheverell preached the Assize sermon at Derby upon the Communication of Sin. On the 5th of November, the anniversary of the Gunpowder Plot and of William's landing at Tor Bay, he discoursed the Lord Mayor at St. Paul's on the perils of false brethren. Both sermons were covert attacks on the Revolution, and the second was the less covert of the two. In it he went so far as to designate Lord Treasurer Godolphin, not obscurely, by the nickname of Volpone, the scoundrel in Ben Jonson's familiar comedy. The Lord Mayor was a Tory, a High Churchman, and a member of Parliament. He was so much delighted with the preacher that he took him home to dinner, and begged him to print the sermon. He even moved the Court of Aldermen to make a formal request in that sense. The aldermen refused. But Sacheverell took his patron's advice, and sold forty thousand copies.

Few less interesting persons than Henry Sacheverell have ever intruded themselves into the pages of history. But when Macaulay talks of a foolish parson, and Lord Stanhope refers to "the buzz of a single insignificant priest," they overshoot the mark. Sacheverell was not a fool. Nor was he in his own time and place altogether insignificant. He was a popular preacher, verbose and rhetorical, but quite capable of expressing himself in a forcible manner, and of appealing to sentiments which thousands shared. The Act of Settlement, and the Protestant Succession, were by no means secure. The Queen's life was a bad one. Her misfortunes as a mother had weakened her health, and she was prone to indulgence in the pleasures of the table. She was a childless widow, not likely to marry again, nor to have children if she did. The heir to the throne by statute was a German woman unknown in England, though she happened to be the grand-daughter of James the First. Her son George was as un-English as herself, a brave soldier, it is true, but a man of detestable character who kept his wife in perpetual imprisonment, while he consorted with ugly and rapacious harlots. The Queen's throne was probably safe so long as she herself lived. But who could say what would happen if she died, or when the Act of Settlement might be repealed? If the Pretender was not less French than the Elector was German, his habits were not repulsive, and he had the manners of a gentleman. James had many friends in England, who would be strengthened and encouraged by such exhortations as Sacheverell's. Early in December 1709 the Cabinet met to consider what should be done about the sermon. The Queen thought that it was a very bad one, and that the doctor well deserved to be punished. No one proposed that it should be treated with the contemptuous indifference recommended by Macaulay and Stanhope, writing at their ease in quiet times. The question before the Cabinet was whether Sacheverell should be prosecuted by the Attorney General in a Court of Law, or impeached by the House of Commons and tried by the House of Lords. Somers was for prosecution, Sunderland was for impeachment. Godolphin sided with Sunderland, and Sacheverell was impeached. The opinion of Somers is not lightly to be dismissed. But on the other hand we have the deliberate, considered judgment of the greatest constitutional theorist who wrote in English, Edmund Burke. Although Burke was not born till twenty years after Sacheverell's impeachment, he was nursed in the creed of the English Revolution, and the Whigs of 1688 were the fathers of his Church. In his Appeal from the New to the Old Whigs, he says, "It rarely happens to a Party to have the opportunity of a clear, authentic, recorded declaration of their political tenets upon the subject of a great constitutional event like that of the Revolution. The Whigs had that opportunity, or, to speak more properly, they made it. The impeachment of Dr. Sacheverell was undertaken by a Whig Ministry and a Whig House of Commons, and carried on before a prevalent and steady majority of Whig Peers. It was carried on for the purpose of condemning the principles on which the Revolution was first opposed, and afterwards calumniated, in order, by a juridicial sentence of the highest authority, to confirm and fix Whig principles as they operated both in the resistance to King James and in the subsequent settlement; and to fix them in the extent and with the limitations with which it was meant they should be understood by posterity." These are weighty words, and so are those in which Burke describes the managers of the impeachment. "They were not," says he, "umbratiles doctors, men who had studied a free constitution only in its anatomy and upon dead systems." Unlike most writers on constitutional law, "they knew it alive and in action." It was not the punishment of Dr. Sacheverell that the Cabinet desired, but the authoritative repudiation of his doctrines by Parliament, and the implied guarantee of a Parliamentary title already vested in the House of Hanover.

Before the end of the year Sacheverell had been impeached by the Commons, and ordered into the custody of the Serjeant-at-arms. When he was transferred in due course to Black Rod, the Lords admitted him to bail, and fixed his trial for the 27th of February, 1710, in Westminster Hall. The trial lasted for three weeks, and absorbed public attention in a manner highly flattering to Sacheverell. It was the happiest time of the doctor's life. Nothing pleased him more than to be the cynosure of every eye; and as he drove each day from the chambers he occupied in the Temple to Westminster Hall, crowds of admirers surrounded his coach, shouting for the Church and Sacheverell, or, in still more agreeable phraseology, for Sacheverell and the Church. Colley Cibber mentions in his Autobiography that the trial withdrew numbers from the Opera at the Haymarket. When the Queen went privately without state in her sedan chair to hear the proceedings, the populace expressed without ceremony a hope that she was on the doctor's side. Two eminent divines, Atterbury and Smalridge, with some of Her Majesty's own chaplains, stood by Sacheverell in the Hall. She began to perceive that clerical Toryism was unanimously in favour of the accused, and she therefore leaned in that direction herself. The managers for the Commons were judiciously moderate and discreet. One of them, Sir Robert Eyre, Solicitor General, denied that "the resistance at the Revolution could bear any parallel with the execrable murder of the royal martyr, so justly detested by the whole nation." Sacheverell 's counsel, of whom Sir Simon Harcourt was chief, were equally prudent, and the question between the two sides became extremely narrow. Both agreed that obedience was the rule, and refusal to obey the law an exception, which only extreme necessity would justify. It was argued for Sacheverell that exceptions need not be named in sermons; and against him that, if they were ignored, the rule was fundamentally changed. But what the Whigs chiefly valued was the opportunity of laying down in the most public place, and the most authoritative form, the cardinal doctrines of their political faith. These were not at the time popular with the lower orders. While Eyre and Jekyll and Stanhope and Parker were expounding the limits of royalty, and the safeguards of freedom, a London mob were pulling down conventicles and burning the pews. The Lords treated Sacheverell with singular indulgence. Though defended by the ablest counsel, he was allowed to read, on his own behalf and in his own name, a speech which Atterbury had composed for him. It abounded in zeal for the Protestant Succession, which Atterbury would have maintained by restoring the Catholic Pretender. On the 25th of March the Lords gave their verdict upon their honour in response to Lord Chancellor Cowper, who called upon them by their rank, beginning with the junior Baron. By a majority of sixty-nine voices against fifty-two Sacheverell was found guilty of the offence charged against him. Four Bishops, including Burnet of Salisbury, the historian, voted against the doctor. Archbishop Sharp of York, and Bishop Compton of London, were in his favour. Nottingham and the other Tory leaders voted Not Guilty, as a matter of course. Three Whig Dukes, Shrewsbury, Somerset, and Argyll refused to vote with their party, and were regarded with approval by the Court. Shrewsbury pronounced the doctor to be innocent. Somerset stood neutral on the steps of the throne. Argyll, after voting Guilty, voted against the proposed suspension from preaching, which was the only punishment inflicted on Sacheverell. The period was reduced on a division from seven years to three, but it was ordered that the two incriminated sermons should be burnt by the common hangman. Although Godolphin expressed to Marlborough, in rather undignified language, his disappointment at the inadequacy of this result, the Whigs had, as Burke points out, achieved their main and chief object. Their principles had been adopted, and the principles of the Tories had been condemned, by both Houses of Parliament, after a solemn and exhaustive discussion in the great Hall of William Rufus. They could afford to let Sacheverell enjoy his bonfires and illuminations, his progresses and plaudits, even the benefice to which a Tory patron prefer! ed him in Wales. They had vindicated the Revolution and the Constitution by showing that the two words were practically synonymous.

When Parliament was prorogued on the 5th April, 1710, with a speech from the throne advising men "to be quiet and to do their own business rather than busy themselves in reviving questions and disputes of a very high nature," the Whig government seemed unassailable at home and abroad. Marlborough, who was never really a Whig, though he was always a Protestant, reposed upon his military laurels, and took more interest in an unsuccessful attempt to obtain for himself the lucrative Vice-Royalty of the Netherlands, which he had formerly refused, than in the prosecution of Sacheverell. The love of money is not apt to diminish with years, and John Churchill felt it strongly from his callow youth. His wife, who shared it with him, did not share his prudence or his self-control. The day after the prorogation, while her lord was in Holland, she forced herself upon the Queen at Kensington, and poured out a flood of reproachful self-defence. The Duchess was not really a clever woman, and, notwithstanding their long intimacy, she had failed to understand the Queen. Her profoundly sagacious husband, who read men much more easily than he read books, had observed and noted a characteristic trait in James the Second, which was that, at the close of a long argument, his Majesty would repeat his original opinion in precisely the same words. Anne was like her father. Writing before the interview, the Duchess, in order to procure it, promised that it would not require the Queen to give an answer. Her Majesty laid hold of this concession and would by no means let it go. Neither the expostulations of the Duchess nor her tears could elicit from her royal mistress any change in the sullen formula, "You desired no answer, and you shall have none." At last, finding that her angry playmate would not go, Anne herself left the room, and the Duchess saw her no more for ever.

The reign of the first favourite was over, and the ascendency of Mrs. Masham was complete. A few days afterwards. Lord Kent, the Whig Lord Chamberlain, was dismissed, and the Duke of Shrewsbury, who had voted for Sacheverell, received the appointment, without the consent or knowledge of Godolphin. The Lord Treasurer submitted meekly to the affront, and went on betting at Newmarket as if nothing had happened. All this time Marlborough was at the Hague, employed in considering fresh negotiations for peace. He was no longer desirous of continuing a war in which he could gain no glory that he had not already won. His position, and the position of Great Britain, which was due to him, were truly splendid. No English statesman, not even Cromwell, would have thought it possible in the seventeenth century for any European power or concert of powers, to prevail over the combination of France and Spain. The eighteenth century was but ten years old, and the proudest of French sovereigns was humbly suing England for peace on any terms, short of compelling his grandson by arms to surrender the Spanish throne. England, however, was in the hands of her allies, with whom she could not decently break, and the Dutch insisted that Louis should drink the cup of humiliation to the dregs. When he declined, the Peace Conference, held at Gertruydenberg, broke up, and the campaign was once more renewed. Marlborough was now master of the situation. The Marshals of France retired at his approach, and would not give him battle. He passed their lines without losing a man, and invested Douay, which had a garrison of eight thousand troops. Assisted by Eugene, he prevented Villars, whose headquarters were at Cambray, from marching to its relief, and on the 25th of June Douay capitulated. It began to look as if Calais would once more fall into English hands, when a political convulsion in England itself changed the whole aspect of affairs. Emboldened by the pusillanimity of Godolphin, the Queen went a step further, and removed from her counsels a much more important person than the Marquis of Kent. This was the Earl of Sunderland, Marlborough's son-in-law, and Secretary of State. Sunderland was in theory a violent Whig, his enemies said a Republican, obnoxious to the Queen for his temper no less than for his principles. In fact he was used by the Jacobites, and not unwilling to serve them. His successor, appointed through Godolphin, but without consulting him, was Lord Dartmouth, a Tory, a High Churchman, and something very like a

Jacobite himself. That Marlborough should retain his command, despite the insult to his family, was natural and proper. His country was still at war, and he was worth a hundred thousand men. But Godolphin, and even Somers, showed on this occasion a spirit unworthy of themselves. For, though the doctrine of collective responsibility was not then established, and it was not yet regarded as essential that a Cabinet should be wholly Whig, or wholly Tory, two such nominations as Shrewsbury's and Dartmouth's amounted to a withdrawal of the Queen's confidence from her Whig advisers. They were designed to express her disapproval of Sacheverell's impeachment. They were directed against Godolphin and Marlborough. They were known to have been prompted by Mrs. Masham, and through Mrs. Masham by Harley. The Tories, the country party, were delighted, and assured poor distracted Anne that she was now Queen indeed. The Whigs, the moneyed party, were alarmed, and the Governor of the Bank headed a deputation of protest to the Queen. They got a short dry answer to the effect that they had nothing to fear from "any further changes" which might be made.

Sunderland had been dismissed on the 13th of June. But it was not till the 8th of August that the Queen struck her great blow. On that day, taking advantage of some uncourtly words employed by the Lord Treasurer at a Council in her Majesty's presence, she ordered Godolphin to break his staff, the symbol of office, promising him at the same time a pension of four thousand a year. Godolphin was sixty-five, and old for his age. Although he had clung to his post as long as he decently could, and perhaps longer, he retired with dignity, and without unmanly complaints. Had it not been for his pension, he would have been a poor man. In a corrupt age he was incorruptible, and the finances of this country never had a more vigilant steward. He would spend money freely where it was required, and his name must always be coupled with Marlborough's in joint responsibility for campaigns which were not less providently organized than they were brilliantly designed and splendidly achieved. His financial administration, assailed by unscrupulous opponents, was so conclusively defended by Walpole, that the malice of his critics was put to silence and to shame. Walpole himself soon followed his chief into retirement. It had not, however, come to be acknowledged that there was any head of the Government except the Queen, and the removal of Godolphin did not of itself destroy his Cabinet. The Treasury was put into Commission with a titled nonentity as First Lord, and Robert Harley as

Chancellor of the Exchequer. But Harley became in effect Prime Minister, and proceeded to reconstruct the Ministry. Harley's principles were fluid. Brought up a Whig and a Nonconformist, he had become a Tory and a Churchman. He was, however, a moderate Churchman, and a lukewarm Tory. His Toryism indeed chiefly consisted in a desire to stand well with Mrs. Masham and the Queen. Having got what he wanted for himself, he tried his hand at a coalition. He induced John Holles, Duke of Newcastle, uncle of the notorious placeman, to remain Lord Privy Seal. He made fruitless overtures to Halifax. He did his best to keep Somers, Cowper, and especially Walpole. But, finding that they were not prepared to act with him, and did not believe in his strange professions of being a Whig at bottom, he turned them out, and presented Anne with the Tory Cabinet which was her heart's desire. Harcourt became Lord Chancellor in the room of Cowper, Rochester, the Queen's uncle, succeeded Somers as Lord President, and Ormond was declared Lord Lieutenant of Ireland instead of Wharton. With Wharton fell his Chief Secretary, Joseph Addison, the best and most popular representative of Whiggery in the world of letters. The new Secretary of State was Henry St. John, Harley's principal confederate, a man of boundless and unscrupulous ambition, whose real aim was to exclude the House of Hanover from the throne of England.

Even before her Tory Cabinet was complete, and while Cowper still held the Great Seal, the Queen, on the 21st of September, 1710, dissolved the Parliament of 1708. This assertion of her prerogative, though it would not now be regarded as constitutional, was justified by the result. The Tories and High Churchmen, on whose behalf she was acting, carried everything before them, insomuch that their majority in the new House of Commons was estimated at four to one. It is strange, as Macaulay says, that an Administration judicious in its policy at home, and glorious for its exploits abroad, should have been assailed with a roar of obloquy, and defeated with an emphasis of ignominy, which would have seemed appropriate if Louis were the arbiter of Europe, and Marlborough had suffered defeat. The explanation of the paradox is not easy, even if there be added to the popularity of Sacheverell the unpopularity of the war. There was no enthusiasm for the Queen, for Harley, or for St. John. Impatience of taxation, and disgust with the Allies, especially with the Dutch, may have done something for the Tories. But the Church undoubtedly did far more. The cry of "Low Church is no Church" was more effective than it had been at any time since the Revolution. The country party, who resorted to general and unscrupulous intimidation of electors, were zealous against Whigs, Dissenters, and the moneyed interest of the towns. They had no confidence in Marlborough, and though they called themselves Protestants, many of them were Jacobites at heart. The Whigs in those days were better patriots than the Tories, for Tory hatred of the Allies had in 1710 reached a pitch at least as high as Whig hatred of Napoleon's enemies rose during the first ministry of Pitt.

No sooner had the new Parliament met on the 25th of November, than the Queen declared herself for the Protestant Succession and the House of Hanover. Yet in the early months of 1711 Harley and St. John employed a French Catholic priest, Gaultier by name, to negotiate secretly with the King of France and the Pretender for the conclusion of peace, if not for something more. While the House of Commons was voting six millions for a continuance of the war, and Marlborough was again at the Hague, planning fresh manoeuvres, this dark and sinister plot was conducted by the Queen's confidential servants in the Queen's own name. De Torcy, the French Minister for Foreign Affairs, was assured that Anne had the most tender feelings for her brother James, and that Harley wished the Pretender to come by his own upon the next demise of the Crown. Few more disgraceful episodes besmirch the pages of English history, and the final touch of infamy is added by a recommendation that the Archduke Charles, the ally of Great Britain, should be kept by French Generals within the walls of Barcelona. Different indeed was the management of British diplomacy and war under Harley and St. John from what it had been under Marlborough and Godolphin. While the principal Ministers of the Queen, her "prime ministers," as they were called in the plural, coquetted with the Pretender, and caballed against the allies of Great Britain, a British General, James Stanhope, who had served under the illustrious Duke, was compelled by no fault of his own to capitulate to Marshal Vendome at Brihuega in Spain, and become a prisoner of France. But Stanhope, founder of the Earldom, was a Whig, and in the rage of party spirit which then prevailed the Tories regarded his discomfiture as a triumph for themselves. The temper in which they had accepted office is described with entire candour by St, John. "I am afraid," he wrote, "that we came to court by the same dispositions as all parties have done; that the principal spring of our actions was to have the government of the State in our hands; that our principal views were the conservation of this power, great employments to ourselves, and great opportunities of rewarding those who had helped to raise us, and of hurting those who stood in opposition to us."

The German historian von Ranke has expressed an opinion that, in the last four years of Queen Anne's reign, during the Cabinet of Harley and St. John, lies its real historic importance. That is to confound the transitory with the permanent part of human affairs. Tory predominance from 1710 to 1714, described in the feeble apologetics of an author who usurped the famous name of Swift, was no more than the prelude to the Whig ascendency of the first two Georges. This period has attained a fascinating, but a delusive, celebrity, from the number of great writers who dignified by their genius its pitiful intrigues. As statesmen, Harley and St. John were worse than useless, almost entirely contemptible. As generous and sympathetic friends to men of letters whom they appreciated, and not merely rewarded, they have received from posterity a gratitude too indiscriminate to be just. St. John's own writings, of which Burke fully understood the real value, are still admired by some, and if style were an end in itself, if the art of expression were valuable without reference to the thing expressed, they would be admirable indeed. But though he failed equally to destroy the Christian religion, and to construct a patriot King, St. John was as good a judge of literature as of burgundy, and Harley loved books without adding to their number. In 1710 they both saw the value of enlisting literary support, and they made a notable acquisition. It was the classical age of the political pamphlet, standing between the glorious sunrise of Milton and the splendid sunset of Burke. They found a pamphleteer without eloquence, without romance, without elevation of soul, but with a clearness of intellect, a soundness of judgment, a lucidity of style, a richness of humour, a crushing, penetrating, remorseless irony, which have never been combined in any other writer before or since.

The Reverend Jonathan Swift was then in the forty-fourth year of his age. Though born in Dublin, and educated at Trinity College, Swift always indignantly denied that he was an Irishman. A man, he said, might as well be called a horse because he was born in a stable. He was, however, ordained in Ireland, all his preferments were Irish, and he was in 1710 the incumbent of Laracor, with a prebendal stall in the cathedral church of St. Patrick. It is difficult for any one acquainted with Swift's published works to believe that his Churchmanship, or even his Christianity, was more than nominal. But his personal pride, which early hardships, and the patronage of his kinsman Sir William Temple, had developed to insolent arrogance, made him jealous for the establishment of which he was a minister, the Church of Ireland. It was not the Church of the Irish people, most of whom were Catholics, while many in the north were Presbyterians. It was the Church of the English Pale, and it was only for the Pale in Ireland that Swift really cared. The Irish Catholics were in his eyes scarcely human, though he relieved, with a generosity in honourable contrast to his personal penuriousness, the necessities of the Dublin poor. The Irish Presbyterians were dangerous enemies, to be fought by tests in lieu of faggots. The Protestant Episcopal Church was his own; and he stood up for its rights, real or imaginary, as a soldier maintains the honour of his regiment. The Tale of a Tub, which appeared in 1704, had already made him famous. For though, like almost all his writings, it was anonymous, the secret had not been kept, and connoisseurs were aware that the poor parson was a power. Swift had no political principles, and he had become intimate with the Whigs in 1707, when he tried his best to arrange for the participation of the Irish Protestant Church in Queen Anne's Bounty. They had not, however, rewarded him in any substantial manner, and he was a perilous ally for them, because he could not be civil to Dissenters. There were indeed few people to whom he could be civil. Incapable of the passions which soften human nature, though they may corrupt it, he was a prey to envy, hatred, malice, and all uncharitableness. Although he liked clever women, and they liked him, he was in truth a real misanthrope, and his mind was full of loathsome images, which he loved to delineate for the benefit of his less fortunate fellow-creatures. A more manly side of his character was his vaulting ambition, which by 1710 had estranged him from the ungrateful Whigs, and prepared him for the reception of St. John's flattery. In November of that year he became a contributor to the Tory Examiner, and wrote for it regularly till June 1711. His principal colleagues were Prior and Defoe. His chief opponents were Addison and Steele. Not one of them could in controversy hold a candle to him. Time, which displays the true proportions of things, exhibits the reign of Anne as dominated by Marlborough and by Swift. Neither of them had any nobility of soul. Both were time-servers and self-seekers. But these are moral deficiencies. Intellectual faults they had none. At the very time when Swift had made himself the slave of a party, when he was writing for his employers two of his masterpieces. The Conduct of the Allies, and A Letter to the October Club, he appeared, so consummate is his art, to be simply putting plain good sense into good plain English. His triumph, and the triumph of his employers, was short. But, while it lasted, it was complete, and to no man were they more indebted than they were to him. They did not really trust him. He was not, as he fondly imagined, in their secrets. With all his faults he was a truthful man, and they wisely kept him in ignorance of their clandestine communications with the Pretender, so that he might deny what he did not know. He proved a wonderfully dexterous, and an infinitely useful, agent. Macaulay has written on the margin of his Swift that a man must have been behind the scenes in politics to appreciate the excellence of the Letter to the October Club. It is indeed a storehouse of practical sagacity, and it had the desired result of quieting those Tory highfliers who expected all things in an hour, whose minds were clouded by their October beer, who believed that Harley was one of themselves, and that St. John was a High Churchman, meaning what he said.

When Harley and St. John, who were at this time on familiar and intimate terms, had secured the services of Swift, they made up their minds to get rid of Marlborough. He was their most dangerous enemy, as Swift was their most valuable friend. But it was necessary to proceed against him with extreme caution, for his treasons were imperfectly known, and his achievements had dazzled the eyes of mankind. When he arrived in London, between the Christmas of 1710 and the New Year of 1711, the popular cheers which greeted him were mingled with more ominous shouts of "No Popery," and "No wooden shoes," such as the French were supposed to wear while attending their confessionals, and eating their frogs. At Court he was not in favour. The Queen received him coldly, although he showed the inherent baseness which even the splendour of his genius cannot hide by the servility of his adulation, and by, an offer that his wife should not so much as come into the Royal presence, if only she might be allowed to keep her official emoluments. The Queen, having fallen completely under the influence of Mrs. Masham, and through her of Harley, refused to be conciliated, and peremptorily demanded from the Duchess her golden key. It is painful to add that on the 17th of January, 1711, the first soldier of the age, perhaps of any age, fell on his knees before a peevish woman, and passionately begged that his wife might not be dismissed. The one excuse to be suggested for him, strange and paradoxical as it may seem, is that he was really and truly afraid of the Duchess. He had to go home, and tell her that he had failed, whereupon she characteristically threw the key at his head. She received, without a murmur from the Queen, the lavish pecuniary compensation which she was not ashamed to demand. But her kingdom was taken from her, and divided among the Medes and Persians. The Duchess of Somerset, whose husband, though a Whig, was an early friend of the Queen's, and had not voted against Sacheverell, became Mistress of the Robes, while Mrs. Masham, who had done it all, was made Keeper of the Privy Purse. Elizabeth, Duchess of Somerset, wife of "the proud Duke," the last of the original Percys, was satirized by Swift in the Windsor Prophecy as "carrots from Northumberland." The Tories were afraid of her influence over the Queen, and of her intrigues with the Whigs. Marlborough, whom the Somersets hated, continued to be Captain General, though not for life, and on the 18th of February, 1711, he sailed for the Hague to consult with Heinsius about the renewal of the war.

The Government were seeking an opportunity to abandon the European alliance, and to make peace with France. If they had openly and avowedly, with the knowledge of the Empire and of the States General, made overtures of peace, their conduct would have deserved rather praise than blame. Louis the Fourteenth had ceased to be a danger, or even a bugbear. Great Britain was in a position to dictate her own terms, for Marlborough had placed her on a pinnacle of greatness which even Cromwell scarcely reached. But honest statesmen, Somers for instance, or Walpole, would have made a point of acting with Austria and Holland until it became clear that those Powers would not accept a reasonable arrangement. Harley and St. John, on the contrary, behaved as if England's allies were her enemies, as if her enemies were her friends, and as if the Pretender were her lawful king. They relied upon the undoubted and by no means surprising fact that the war had become extremely unpopular. If Southey had written his poem about Malplaquet, instead of Blenheim, the reason would have been at least as good as the rhyme. After Ramillies there was no sufficient cause for prolonging the struggle, and by 1711 it had become palpably futile. When Lutheran emigrants from the Palatinate, "poor Palatines" as they were called, received public money to establish them in Ireland and in the North American Colonies, while many Englishmen were suffering severely from distress, popular discontent became vociferous, and Marlborough's name no longer served to allay the tumult. The House of Commons, which in 1711 was more like Convocation than it has ever been before or since, protested against the importation of these destitute aliens on the ground, amongst others, that by multiplying Dissenters it endangered the Church. Even the impeachment of Sunderland, who as Secretary of State had brought them in, was proposed. But Sunderland was no longer in office, and the matter was allowed to drop.

Harley might have found some difficulty in retaining a position which the more impetuous Tories would gladly have transferred to St. John, if an unforeseen accident had not suddenly made him a popular hero. A French exile residing in London, the Marquis de Guiscard, who had given valuable information to Marlborough and Godolphin at earlier stages of the war, demanded money from Harley, which that prudent financier refused to pay. Guiscard thereupon wrote to the French court disclosing what he knew, and was arrested by order of St. John, who discovered his treachery, on the 8th of March, 1711. Brought before the Privy Council at the Cockpit in Whitehall, Guiscard suddenly rushed at Harley, and stabbed him in the breast with a penknife. The wound was slight, and it was Guiscard who died, by the swords of St. John and other Privy Councillors. But Harley was laid up for some weeks with fever, and the calm courage which he displayed under the murderous attack, as by intention it had undoubtedly been, was in the mouths of all men. The rival claims of St. John were forgotten, and Harley became without dispute the first Minister of the Crown.

Never was there a more loyal House of Commons, nor one more devoted to the landed interest. Soldiers, courtiers, merchants, and, above all, Dissenters were the objects of its jealousy and distrust. Parliament enacted in this year that every knight of the shire, or county member, must possess an income of six hundred pounds a year, and every burgess, or borough member, an income of three hundred pounds a year, from land. It was also ordered by the Queen's special and earnest desire, that fifty new churches should be built in London, from the produce of the civic duty on coal, as recommended by the Lower House of Convocation through their Jacobite Prolocutor, Francis Atterbury. As if still further to exhibit the political influence of the Church, a Bishop, Robinson of Bristol, was at the same time admitted to the Cabinet as Lord Privy Seal. Robinson, in the course of his unusual career, had been for a quarter of a century chaplain to the Swedish Embassy at Stockholm, had discharged the duties of Minister during the Minister's absence, and had actually accompanied Charles the Twelfth to Norway, while he held a benefice in England.

Harley had now reached the height of his power. On the 26th of April, 1711, he reappeared in the House of Commons after his illness, and received the congratulations of the Speaker. A few days afterwards he made his financial statement as Chancellor of the Exchequer, and proposed, without a glimmer of light on the real nature of what he was doing, the incorporation of the South Sea Company. A month later he was gazetted Earl of Oxford, reviving the ancient title of the De Veres, which had become extinct less than ten years before, and on the blessed anniversary of the glorious Restoration he took the oaths as Lord Treasurer before Simon Harcourt, Lord Keeper. Meanwhile there had occurred on the Continent a great change. How much the history of the eighteenth century was affected by the smallpox would be an interesting subject of investigation. In April 1711 it carried off the French Dauphin, who was soon followed by his son and the Emperor Joseph, a young man of thirty-two. Joseph was succeeded, with the consent of the Electors, by his brother Charles, the candidate of the Allies for the throne of Spain. The ironic texture of human affairs, on which great satirists have exhausted their vocabularies, was seldom illustrated in a more grimly practical way. Even those who objected most strongly to the aggrandisement of the Bourbons did not desire to see Spain a fief of the Empire, as she had been in the days of Charles the Fifth, and no further attempt was made to disturb Philip of Anjou. The old King of France, who had reduced his country from the heights of glory to the depths of degradaion, was left to enjoy such comfort as he could derive from the fact that his grandson now reigned without dispute over a country not less humbled than his own.

The campaign of 1711, though for political reasons it led to no tangible result, was not less illustrative of Marlborough's military genius than the battle of Blenheim itself. He planned with Prince Eugene a great project for invading French territory from Tournay. Eugene, however, was recalled, by orders issued from Vienna, to guard the Imperial Electors at Frankfort, and Marlborough had to act alone against Marshal Villars, who was so proud of his defensive lines that he called them, in the spirit of King Canute, his ne plus ultra. Marlborough watched the Marshal's designs with calm disdain, and was no more impeded by them than the ocean was impeded by Canute. When the time had come, in the month of August, he crossed the Schelde, and besieged the garrison of Bouchain, which he took, with three thousand prisoners, on the 12th of September. The French were in numbers far stronger than the English army, and there was not another soldier in Europe who would have regarded Marlborough's enterprise as feasible with the men at his disposal. This achievement relaxed the Queen's purse-strings, which had been closed since her quarrel with the

Duchess, and she gave another sum of twenty thousand pounds towards the completion of Blenheim Palace.

Marlborough never asked advice, and seldom took it, being indeed accustomed to receive it with the one word of comment, "Silly." But he did announce his intentions at this juncture to his old colleague Godolphin, who had never failed him. At the same time, with the serene, high-bred courtesy so much admired by Chesterfield, he furnished special protection at Cateau-Cambresis to the diocesan estates of the illustrious Archbishop Fenelon. Whatever he may have been below, Marlborough was always on the surface a great gentleman. But the position of this singular and incomparable personage was being steadily undermined by intriguers, who resembled him only in the want of scruple and of shame. The Duchess had been banished from the Court, and the "all-accomplished St. John" was pulling every wire within his reach to compass the ruin of the Protestant Succession in the person of its champion. He and Lord Oxford, who for this purpose, though his nominal superior, was his actual tool, sent Matthew Prior the poet on a secret mission to King Louis and de Torcy at Fontainebleau. The Queen objected to the social grade of the envoy as too low for such an office. But Prior, now known as a graceful and rather licentious author of familiar verse, was by profession a diplomatist, had been Secretary to the English Embassy at Paris, and had taken a leading part in negotiating the Treaty of Ryswick for King William. The motives of his journey to France in the summer of 1711 were carefully concealed from the public, and even Swift, who thought he knew everything, had no knowledge of them at all. If secrecy had been confined to England, it would need no excuse. Even in our own day, when the light of publicity beats upon many things not thought proper in the eighteenth century to be divulged, the preliminary stages of an international agreement cannot always be communicated to the Press. What makes the authors of these particular negotiations infamous is the deceit they practised upon Britain's allies. Swift's argument in his famous pamphlet, that we undertook more than our share of the burden involved in the war, while Holland and the Empire derived more than their share of the profit, is a perfectly fair one. But he was allowed to write in ignorance of the facts. He had no idea that while he was defending Ministers, they were doing what he could not have defended. So far as the requirements of this country alone were concerned, their proposals were reasonable enough. The greatest of British interests at that time was peace. St. John was entitled to say that, if the Spanish crown were always separated from the French, a Bourbon might be suffered, as Philip the Fifth, to reign at Madrid. Prior was instructed to demand, in return for this concession, Gibraltar, Port Mahon, and Newfoundland for Great Britain; the sinister privilege of the Asiento, or right of supplying the Spanish Colonies with negro slaves; a guaranteed frontier on the Rhine for Austria, and a Barrier Treaty for the Dutch. When Prior returned to London, he was followed by a French envoy, Menager by name, who further undertook on behalf of his master that France should acknowledge the title of Queen Anne, and the validity of the Protestant Succession. At the same time, with a refinement of treachery which may safely be attributed to St. John, a different set of proposals, omitting all the advantages secured by England, was drawn up for communication to the Hague. Holland, however, was most reluctant to accept terms, and the Emperor was furious at the very suggestion of them. The English Whigs took up the cry, and in the month of October 1711 the peacemongers were bitterly lampooned. That the Tory Government were substantially right in their policy would not now be in any quarter denied. There was nothing left in dispute for which a civilized nation could with justice, or even with decency, wage war. Not the thing done, but the manner of doing it, has left an indelible stain upon the characters of Oxford and St. John. Oxford's nature was crooked, and St. John preferred, whenever he had a choice, to accomplish his objects by dishonest means.

When Marlborough, returning, as usual, from the Hague, landed at Greenwich on the anniversary of Queen Elizabeth's accession, the 17th of November, there were popular demonstrations in London against the Pope and the Pretender. Although Marlborough wisely avoided them, and the Government treated the demonstrators with foolish severity, the Whigs were not discouraged, but resolved to find an opportunity for turning the Ministry out. In the House of Commons the Tory majority was too strong for them, and they therefore directed their attention to the House of Lords, which had not then lost its control over executive affairs. The balance of power among the Peers was held at that time by Nottingham, who resented his exclusion from office, and was willing to coalesce with the Whigs, if they would help him in enforcing upon Dissenters a regular, and not merely an occasional, conformity to the Established Church. The ignominious bargain was struck, and the aid of Marlborough was secured to protest against Spain, with her West Indian possessions, being left to the House of Bourbon. The Elector of Hanover, who had an envoy in London,

Baron Bothmar, allowed it to be known that he, who after his mother was heir to the British crown, shared the Duke of Marlborough's views. On the other hand the Queen, as became a woman, was sincerely anxious to stop the further effusion of blood. When Parliament met on the 7th of December, the Speech from the Throne was earnestly pacific. Nottingham met it with an amendment which, immediately and directly, raised the question of Spain and the Bourbons. He was supported by all the Whigs, including Bishop Burnet, except the Duke of Shrewsbury, who went over to the Tories. Marlborough spoke with dignity and power, "in the presence of Her Majesty, of this illustrious assembly, and of that Supreme Being, who is infinitely above all the powers upon earth." His direct reference to the Queen is historically interesting, because Anne was the last Sovereign who attended debates in the House of Lords, as she was the last to exercise the legislative veto, and to preside over meetings of the Cabinet. When Marlborough denounced the peace as dangerous to the political balance of Europe, the effect must have been profound, and Nottingham's amendment was carried by 62 Contents against 54 Not Contents. In the House of Commons the same evening the Ministerial majority exceeded a hundred. Now-a-days, such a conflict between the Houses would injure no one except the Lords themselves; but at the beginning of the eighteenth century the constitutional position was very different. The House of Commons did not really represent the people; and although the Commons could stop a war by refusing supplies, they could hardly treat the Lords with indifference. Too many of them owed their seats to "noble" patrons.

Where the two Houses did agree, their unanimity was disastrous. Nottingham at once exacted the price for his vote against the peace, reintroducing his Occasional Conformity Bill, which he had never yet been able to pass. It was carried through the House of Lords with the help of unworthy Whigs, such as Wharton the blasphemer, and welcomed with enthusiasm by the Tory majority in the House of Commons. This odious statute provided that any officer of the army or navy, any Minister of State, any Mayor, Alderman, or Councillor, and any Magistrate, who attended a chapel or religious meeting of Dissenters, should be deprived of his post, and fined forty pounds. The only possible excuse or apology for so grotesque a form of persecution is, that the law which it superseded, was incapable of serious defence. Ever since the Restoration, it had been necessary for all the persons described by the Act to qualify themselves by taking the sacrament in the Church of England, and the "Occasional

Conformity" thus prescribed by law was, not without reason, regarded as scandalous. But to substitute an injustice for a scandal is not an improvement, and the political folly of this legislation was enhanced by the fact that, while many Churchmen were Jacobites, the Nonconformists were, every one of them, loyal to the Act of Settlement. The moral principle of the Occasional Conformity Act, in which the dismal Nottingham sincerely believed, must be judged in the light of St. John's enmity to the Christian religion, though his true sentiments had not then been fully avowed. Although St. John was destitute of political honesty, and of moral courage, there is a daredevil recklessness in his brief official career, which compels a sort of admiration. That such a man as he was should have conceived, and executed, in conjunction with Oxford, the idea of dismissing Marlborough from the public service, reminds one of the two private soldiers who, in the terse language of Tacitus, undertook the task of transferring the Roman Empire, and transferred it. They struck at Marlborough, these little men, in his most vulnerable part, his rapacious avarice.. But even so their case was not a good one. A Tory Commission, appointed by themselves, reported that Marlborough during his campaigns had received large sums of money from a wealthy Jew, Sir Solomon Medina, and from other contractors for supplies. Marlborough admitted the fact, alleging that he had followed the example of previous commanders, and that he had employed the money in obtaining information of the enemy's designs. There can be no doubt that, if the standard of public morality which then prevailed be taken as a standard, this particular charge against Marlborough breaks down. That a general in the field should make money by his position, and should even, like Marlborough, realize a considerable fortune by his military command, is now impossible, almost unthinkable. But the historian has no right, if he passes ethical judgments at all, to incorporate the ideas of his own age with that of which he is writing, and the best proof that Marlborough's acceptance of these perquisites from Sir Solomon Medina implied no special depravity may be found in the fact that similar presents were received without a qualm by his successor the Duke of Ormond, who was as far above him in purity of character, as he was unequal to him in renown. This ostentatious crusade against the illustrious soldier was a fruit of the narrowest partisanship. It was peculiarly mean and low, because it had been carefully kept for the time when the services of the Captain General would be no longer required. Just as a famous and eloquent Professor of Medicine was said to be a very good doctor, if you had nothing the matter with you, because he amused you with anecdotes, and did you no harm, so the Duke of Ormond commanded the Queen's forces with great success and dignity in time of profound peace, when the power of France had been shattered for more than a generation at Blenheim, at Ramillies, at Oudenarde, and at the terrible battle of Malplaquet. Even in the character of Swift, then the unscrupulous tool of Oxford and Bolingbroke, there are few such sinister traits as the tone in which he writes of Marlborough. In his Journal to Stella, the most intimate and the tenderest record of his thoughts, for the 30th of December, 1711, he tells his "dears," Esther Johnson and her companion, Mrs. Dingley, that "the Duke of Marlborough was at court to-day, and nobody hardly (sic) took notice of him." Who cares now what the courtiers of Queen Anne, or even Swift himself, thought of Marlborough? Morally, they were, most of them, quite as bad as he was. His genius has long outsoared the shadow of their night, and remains the most splendid luminary in the martial firmament of England. The day after Swift's entry in his journal Queen Anne herself, inspired by the evil genius of St. John, directed that Marlborough should be "dismissed from all his employment," not as a result of his conviction, but as a preliminary to his trial. This was Jedburgh justice with a vengeance. But Marlborough, whose public career was thus suddenly brought to a premature close, is too great and too bad a man for pity. To condole with him is to insult him. He fell by ignoble hands, the victim of a stupid woman and a knavish intriguer, after he had placed the enemies of England under his feet, and established the Protestant Succession upon an impregnable rock. He retired to enjoy wealth beyond the dreams of a miser, with the consciousness that he had preserved his country and his faith from ruin, in the company of a wife whom he passionately adored. Although the Duchess had the sort of temper which would provoke a saint, and did destroy the doting fondness of the Queen, she never ruffled the imperturbable serenity, or diminished the constant love, of her celebrated, her almost too celebrated, husband.

Simultaneously with Marlborough's disgrace, as the courtiers called it, there appeared in the Gazette the names of twelve new Peers. This bold stroke, also the work of St. John, has been often discussed by constitutional writers as if it were in some mysterious way unconstitutional. No one thought it so at the time. No one who understands the Constitution would call it so now. That Queen Anne was badly advised in making so sudden and decisive a use of her prerogative, is an arguable proposition, or at worst, a defensible paradox. The existence of the prerogative itself, which has never fallen into disuse, was at the root of the kingly commonwealth of England. The fountain of honour has always contained a pipe which may be turned upon the House of Lords. Lord Oxford's Ministry, in which St. John was the leading spirit, desired to conclude peace with France. Their policy, which in principle, if not in method, was sound, had the approval of a large majority in the House of Commons. To bring the two branches of the Legislature into harmony, by lawful means, for a judicious purpose, is a transaction which may be censured by the pedant in his closet, but will receive a ready condonation from all who understand public affairs. With a prudence characteristic of Oxford, though not of St. John, Ministers began their efforts with the Peerage itself. They called up in their fathers' baronies, as the saying is, the sons of two earls. Two other eldest sons of Peers received baronies of their own, and an Irish Peer became a Peer of Great Britain. The Chief Justice of the Common Pleas, Sir Thomas Trevor, and a couple of baronets, left room for only three untitled commoners, who became respectively, without changing their names, Lord Foley, Lord Bathurst, and Lord Masham. Masham was the husband of the Queen's favourite, and he was nothing more. Perhaps he reminded her Majesty of the late Prince George. Some apprehension seems to have been felt lest Lady Masham, once Abigail Hill, should be thought to lower the dignity of a Peeress, by continuing to dress the Queen, for which exalted purpose she sometimes lay on the floor. But Lady Masham was always willing to make herself useful, and the dignity of a Peeress has survived more serious, if not more ludicrous, shocks. Lord Stanhope has recorded the wholesome answer of a country gentleman, to whom one of these things was offered. "No," said he, "this looks like serving a turn. Peers used to be made for services which they have done, but I should be made for services that I am to do." One of these services was very soon required. On the 2nd of January, 1712, the Twelve took the oaths required by law, and were sarcastically asked by Lord Wharton, in one of the few really good Parliamentary jokes, whether they would vote by their foreman. They had to vote that very day. The Queen desired the Lords by message to adjourn till the 14th of January, when the Commons were to meet. This message might plausibly be called unconstitutional, the right of adjournment being a privilege of each House itself. The motion of the Government was, however, carried by a majority of thirteen, with the aid of the Twelve, against the opposition of the Whigs.

When both Houses met on the 14th of January, Prince Eugene had arrived in London, and the Plenipotentiaries had met at Utrecht to arrange the preliminaries of European peace. Eugene could do nothing for Marlborough, to whom he was always consistently devoted, and the Tories attacked him with calumnious insinuations, as engaged in a plot against the Queen, because he was, like his Royal master, the Emperor Charles the Sixth, unfavourable to the French terms. Lord Oxford had the bad taste to describe him in his presence, as the first Captain in Europe. "If I am so," said the chivalrous Prince, "it is because you have removed my superior." The triumphant Tories were carrying everything before them, and Eugene retired to the Hague without the smallest measure of success. The Tory desire for revenge took the ephemeral shape of a zeal for purity, and found a victim in Robert Walpole. The Commissioners of Public Accounts had formally charged Walpole, whose sense of public honour was never nice, though his sense of public duty was always high, with making illicit gains from Scottish contracts for forage, while he held the office of Secretary at War in the Administration of Godolphin. Walpole was not distinguished for personal greed. He was lavish in his expenditure, legitimate or otherwise, and he died, after an unexampled period of office, a comparatively poor man. On this occasion he had gratified a friend at the cost of the country, which would now-a-days be most justly regarded as an unpardonable offence. But in 1712 such vicarious generosity was regarded as venial, if not laudable, and the Tory House of Commons was animated by party rancour, not by public virtue, when it censured him, expelled him, and committed him to the Tower. His constituency, the borough of King's Lynn, at once reelected him, and he issued from his easy confinement a spirited defence, which completely established his honour with his contemporaries, if it cannot altogether vindicate with posterity the whiteness of his soul. "I hope," wrote Swift to Stella on the 17th of January, 1712, "I hope Walpole will be sent to the Tower, and expelled the House." Swift's amiable desire was gratified. But in later years, when Swift was eating out his heart with mordant bitterness on Irish soil, and giving to himself even more pain than he gave to others, he must often have cursed not only, as we know he did, the day of his birth, but the day when he made an enemy of the mighty Minister whom his fiery darts were powerless to reach. With Walpole was expelled the Duke of Marlborough's secretary, Adam Cardonnel, Member for Southampton. Lord Townshend, who had negotiated the Barrier Treaty, was declared an enemy to the

Queen and kingdom. Marlborough himself, in a published reply to his accusers, said with dignity, and what is more, with truth, "The Commissioners may have observed very rightly that, by the strictest inquiry they could make, they cannot find that any English general ever received this perquisite. But I presume to say the reason is that there was never any other English general, besides myself, who was Commander-in-Chief in the Low Countries." Marlborough was always plausible, and relied much upon the secrecy in which his most scandalous transactions were buried. Justly and widely suspected as he was, his worst villainies were not unearthed until he had passed beyond the reach of all human tribunals, except the court of the historian.

The Parliament of 1710 was chiefly concerned in asserting and establishing the supremacy of Episcopalian Protestantism in general, and of the English Church in particular. The Occasional Conformity Act, an eternal discredit to the Whigs who voted for it in the House of Lords, disqualified all honest Dissenters for political and municipal office. Roman Catholics were of course excluded from Parliament by the Test Act, and Anglo-Catholics had not been heard of. Scottish Presbyterians could not be prevented from sitting in a Legislature not merely English, but British, and to interfere directly with the Presbyterian Church of Scotland would have been to destroy the Union. St. John had no religion of his own, and was incapable of understanding what other people meant by the term. He took his idea of a parson from Swift, and supported High Churchmen, such as Atterbury, because they were Jacobites, or political allies. Scottish Episcopalians were under the peculiar protection of the Ministry, and that they needed the secular arm even so patriotic an historian of his own country as John Hill Burton does not deny. A clerk in holy orders, a minister of the Established Church of Ireland, one Greenshields, settled in Edinburgh, and read to his voluntary congregation the English Liturgy, as he had a perfect right to do. That beautiful service had seldom been heard by the Presbyterians of Scotland since Laud foolishly tried to force it upon them, and the Presbytery of Edinburgh, to whom religious toleration meant tampering with the accursed thing, forbade Greenshields, as an unqualified intruder, to read or preach within the bounds. When he disregarded their prohibition, they brought him before the magistrates, who sent him, like Paul and Silas, to gaol. This truly monstrous sentence, alike illegal and unchristian, was upheld by the Court of Session, the supreme embodiment of justice in Scotland. A Scottish House of Lords, to whom a "remeid of law," in English an appeal, would have lain, no longer existed, having been destroyed by the Act of Union. The British House of Lords, containing bishops, then an abomination to the Scottish mind, having ostensibly inherited the powers of the Scottish Peers, reversed the judgment pronounced at Edinburgh. The devil was thus let loose, and Episcopal clergymen in Scotland were rabbled by the mob. Parliament naturally and properly passed an Act for their protection at the hands of the sheriffs, aided by the secular forces of the Crown. But unfortunately, through sheer ignorance, or perhaps by way of wanton insult, the Presbyterian ministers were directed by this statute to pray in express words for Queen Anne and the Electress Sophia. There could hardly be a better example of the provincial arrogance and stupidity with which Englishmen are sometimes charged. The Presbyterians were as much attached as any Church of England man could be to the Protestant Succession, and they would naturally have prayed for it, if they had been left to themselves. But that Parliament should prescribe their prayers was in their eyes a profane aggression of the secular power upon sacred things, far more important than any title to any throne on earth. The Act became even more obnoxious than it otherwise would have been, because it was accompanied by another statute, which revived the rights of private patrons, who had not commuted them under the Act of 1690, to appoint parochial ministers without the consent of the local presbytery, known as an "harmonious call." And as if this were not enough to disgust the people of Scotland with that Treaty of Union which it should have been the business of Parliament by every available method to commend, the House of Lords had unconstitutionally, if not illegally, refused to admit the Duke of Hamilton after he had been created Duke of Brandon in the Peerage of Great Britain, alleging forsooth, in defiance of recognized and undoubted Prerogative, that the Crown could not confer British Peerages upon Scottish Peers. If the Government of Oxford and St. John wished to make Scotland disloyal, they certainly went the right way to work.

Through his Plenipotentiaries at Utrecht the French King made this year proposals, probably not meant to be final, which excited alarm at the Hague, and indignation in England. Lille and Tournay were to be given him in return for the demolition of his fortress at Dunkirk. He wanted his own barrier in the Netherlands, a very different barrier from Lord Townshend's. Even the Queen's title, as good as his own, except in the eyes of unpopular and discredited Jacobites, he would not condescend to acknowledge, until peace, on his own terms, had been finally concluded. The Dutch Ministers, with timely wisdom and judicious foresight, caused these arrogant demands to be published in their Gazette, and they were thus speedily known in England, where the Tory, semi-Jacobite Cabinet would willingly have concealed them. The wrath of the Whigs at the news was shared by many patriotic Tories, and notwithstanding the new Peers, Charles Montagu, Earl of Halifax, carried unanimously on the 12th of February, a hostile motion in the House of Lords, which Lord Oxford, the most prudent of men, durst not oppose. Misfortune fell at the same time, and fell heavily, upon the House of Bourbon. The very day on which Halifax carried his Resolution the Dauphiness, Marie of Savoy, Duchess of Burgundy, died of measles, and within a fortnight she was followed to the grave by her husband, the heir to the throne of France. Their eldest son expired on the 8th of March, and the succession devolved upon the King's great-grandson, a sickly, unwholesome child, afterwards infamous as Louis the Fifteenth, next to whom by French law came Philip the Fifth, King of Spain. England renewed preparations for war. She had chosen, or her Ministers had chosen for her, to discard the most universally victorious of all her soldiers, and in April they made themselves the laughing-stock of Europe by appointing the Duke of Ormond to be General in Flanders, and to join Prince Eugene at Tournay. Eugene, a great soldier, and as true to Marlborough as the dial to the sun, wished to resume the great project of his former colleague, to fight Marshal Villars, and to invade the heart of France. But Louis the Fourteenth, though he could afford to despise such a commander as Ormond, knew well the capacity of Eugene, was conscious of the evil plight to which, since 1704, his own army had been reduced, and perceived the necessity of making more acceptable overtures. De Torcy was directed to inform St. John that Philip should never become King of France, unless he expressly renounced, both for himself and for his descendants, the crown of Spain. The King of Portugal was suggested as Spanish monarch in Philip's room, for no one anticipated that the baby Louis would survive to make the French Revolution salutary and inevitable. St. John replied that this would not do, and that Philip's renunciation of either the French or the Spanish Crown, instead of being left for the future, as a likely cause of another war, must be put at once into the Treaty of Pease. Louis agreed to this proposal, with some unimportant reservations, and on the loth of May Ormond was directed from London to suspend hostilities till the receipt of further orders. With characteristic treachery, St. John concealed the issue of these instructions from the Dutch Government, the faithful ally of this country, and even the loyal, gallant, honourable Eugene was left to find them out for himself. Eugene, however, was not easily foiled, and he insisted so warmly upon the duty of investing Le Quesnoy, that Ormond could not decently refuse his co-operation. In the British Parliament the Whigs, small in number as they were, at least in the House of Commons, warmly protested against these transactions, and Ministers were reduced to the subterfuge of maintaining that a siege might be lawful, though a battle was not. In the House of Lords Marlborough poured just contempt upon St. John's nefarious design, and Oxford only escaped defeat by telling the deliberate falsehood that the Allies were satisfied with their own betrayal. "We got a great victory last Wednesday," Swift wrote to Stella on the 31st of May, 1712, "we got a great victory last Wednesday in the House of Lords by a majority, I think, of twenty-eight (Contents 40, Not Contents 68), and the Whigs had desired their friends to bespeak places to see Lord Treasurer (the Earl of Oxford) carried to the Tower." The second part of the sentence is not of course seriously meant. But the victory was hardly to be called a moral one; and if the Tower were the proper receptacle for traitors, it would have been no unsuitable lodging for Swift's patrons.

Having the support of both Houses, the Queen's Ministers pursued their isolated policy, in itself a breach of good faith, and on the 6th of June concluded for two months a separate armistice with France in the Netherlands. The Duke of Ormond, who loved peace, and ensued it, willingly obeyed his instructions, so far as he could. But Prince Eugene, accustomed to co-operate with a commander of very different calibre from Ormond's, induced the auxiliary forces to leave the British standard, and it was only with twelve thousand men, who under Marlborough would have gone anywhere, and done anything, that Ormond fell back ingloriously upon Dunkirk.

For his share in this despicable business, St. John was raised to the Peerage, and became Viscount Bolingbroke. Lord Morley, in his brilliant sketch of Walpole's character and career, perhaps the best thing of the kind in the English language, condemns St. John as a trifler for thus leaving the real seat of power for the glittering bribe of a title. The whole course of Henry St. John's long and chequered career shows that he was destitute of true courage, and that he lacked all the elements of real greatness. But, in estimating the comparative importance of the two Houses, we must not forget the tremendous revolution effected by the Reform Act of 1832, which enfranchised the middle classes, and abolished the pocket boroughs. Even in 1712, the House of Commons possessed the power of the purse, and the practical control of the Executive Government which that power implies. On the other hand, the collective responsibility of the Cabinet was still in the making, a majority in the Lords was considered essential to a minister, and many members of Parliament were returned by Peers. St. John, however, behaved with his usual servility. In abject letters to the Queen he entreated that the Earldom of Bolingbroke, which had belonged to his family, might be revived in his favour. If he had been on good terms with the Lord Treasurer, it is possible that this request might have been granted. As he had chosen, against the sagacious advice of Swift, to quarrel with Lord Oxford, who had the ear of Lady Masham, and therefore of the Queen, it was refused, and he had to be content, or as content as he ever could be, with a mere Viscounty. Oxford himself received the Order of the Garter, and thus completely asserted his supremacy in the Cabinet, though to call him Prime Minister would be a technical anachronism.

Bolingbroke at once went to Paris, with the double object of courting Madame de Parabere, an easy prey, and of obtaining a general armistice, not confined to the Netherlands, for four months, in which he also succeeded. He did a third thing, by far the worst of the three. He abandoned to the vengeance of King Philip those inhabitants of Catalonia, who, relying on British honour, had fought on Britain's side. In his Public Spirit of the Whigs, as unscrupulous a piece of sophistry as ever appeared, Swift, replying to Steele, vainly attempts an apology for this crime. Where Swift failed, no one else is likely to succeed, and Bolingbroke's treatment of the Catalans lies under the final ban of all impartial historians. The negotiations for peace had really been conducted by a much more useful person than Bolingbroke, Matthew Prior. A treaty, however, could not be ratified by a man of Prior's plebeian rank; and the Duke of Hamilton was appointed Ambassador for that purpose, with secret instructions to bring over the Pretender. All readers of Thackeray's Esmond will remember what became of Hamilton. He was first insulted, and then challenged, by Lord Mohun. Both the duellists were killed in the encounter, and the Duke of Shrewsbury, a magnificent, if not very effective personage, upon whom the Jacobites could not rely, was sent to Paris as Hamilton's successor. Throughout July Prince Eugene, as commander of the Imperial forces, endeavoured to carry on the war with the aid of the Dutch. But there were no British soldiers, and there was no Duke of Marlborough. Eugene had to look helplessly on, while Marshal Villars defeated a Dutch force under Lord Albemarle at Denain on the 24th of July; and from that day the Dutch Republic acceded to the cause of peace. Even Bouchain, which had been taken by Marlborough, was in his absence recovered by Villars. Bolingbroke was at this time in strict secrecy using Gaultier as an instrument, and proposing that the Pretender should be restored to the British throne, on the next demise of the Crown. One reason made his success impossible. James was a strictly honourable and a sincerely religious man, devoid of all shining talents, but as honest as the day, and therefore as unlike Bolingbroke as might be. Nothing would induce him even to contemplate the possibility of changing his faith, and after the disastrous reign of his father the English people, though thousands of them believed in divine right, would not endure the notion of a Catholic Sovereign. The Electress Sophia, a German old enough to be the Queen's mother, was a philosopher, and a disciple of Leibniz, believing in revealed religion no more than Bolingbroke himself. But she had one supreme merit. She was not a "Papist," and her son, as well as her grandson, had fought under Marlborough. The English people cared no more for the House of Hanover than the House of Hanover cared for them. They were resolved at all costs to uphold the Protestant Succession.

In September 1712 died Sidney, Earl of Godolphin, the ablest and most successful financier whom England had known. Godolphin, who began his career under Charles the Second, was a man prone to cynicism, despising most people, and believing, not without reason, that they had their price. But his own hands were clean, he died poor, and he watched the expenditure of public funds with a jealous, honourable care. While he never suffered money to be wasted on trifles, and had an eye for detail which a modern Secretary to the Treasury might envy, he grudged no payment required for success in the French war, so that Marlborough was indebted to him for the perfection of his transport and supplies. He was in truth the one English friend, except Cadogan, that Marlborough had, and it was in one of the Duke's houses that he died. His death determined Marlborough to leave England, which he had raised to the highest pitch of military renown, and where all parties distrusted, as most persons disliked, him. He had always been strangely sensitive to the attacks of anonymous writers, which were becoming more frequent every day. The world was all before him, where to choose, for his wealth was enormous, and his

Duchess would have accompanied him anywhere. With her he sailed to Ostend in November 1712, and after a visit to the Principality of Mindelheim, once his own, fixed his residence at Antwerp early in 1713.

The prospects of peace, improved, or at all events not diminished, by Marlborough's retirement from public affairs, were much assisted by the pen of Arbuthnot, who introduced John Bull, in his lively satires, as the typical name of an Englishman. Although the power and influence of Grub Street, or, in other words, of the political pamphlet and news-sheet, were higher in the reign of Queen Anne than they have ever been, before or since, the Parliament of 1710 was hostile to the Press as an organ of opinion. The Stamp Act of 1712, opposed by authors so celebrated for their genius, and so diverse in their views, as Swift, Addison, and Defoe, retained its bad eminence on the Statute Book for nearly a century and a half. It imposed upon all newspapers and pamphlets the duty of a half-penny for each half-sheet. This tax upon knowledge, or upon ideas, almost ruined a number of journalists, and their fate was wittily described in the Spectator as "the fall of the leaf." It weighed of course most heavily upon the humblest scribblers, and could not seriously affect such a journal as the Spectator, or such a pamphleteer as Dr. Arbuthnot. John Arbuthnot, physician in ordinary to the Queen, was an ardent Tory, a polished, elegant writer, the most delightful of companions, and the most amiable of men. He was not, like Swift, a statesman, and he was content to interpret the opinions which found most favour with the Court. Anne being in 1712 enthusiastically pacific, her doctor was easily induced to publish a satire on the war, which he called Law is a Bottomless Pitt. The secondary title, explaining the scope and purpose of the tract, is, "Exemplified in the case of the Lord Strutt, John Bull, Nicholas Frog, and Lewis Baboon, who spent all they had in a Law Suit." Arbuthnot was incapable of distinguishing between the Europe of 1712 and the Europe of 1704, nor was it any part of his design to appreciate the splendid services of Marlborough. On the main question, whether peace on honourable terms should be made when he wrote, few would now dispute either his arguments or his inference. Marlborough had done, and more than done, his work. All possible danger from France had long passed away, and a continuance of the armed struggle was useless slaughter. Bolingbroke, upon whom, as Secretary of State, the main responsibility for the negotiations fell, was a traitor to the Act of Settlement, if not to his Royal mistress, and had been in treasonable correspondence, through Gaultier, with the Pretender. But, as James remained obstinately Catholic, and as Catholicism was unpopular in Great Britain, Bolingbroke, to whom all religions were alike, gave him up in public, and even pressed, with a vehemence which deceived many of his countrymen, for the immediate departure of the "Chevalier de St. George" from France. James hesitated to comply with a demand ill suited to the dignity of his claims, and Louis, who only persecuted Protestants, shrank from expelling him. At last, on the 17th of February, 1713, Bolingbroke directed Shrewsbury to call for an immediate reply from the French Government, and three days afterwards the Chevalier left Chalons for Bar in Lorraine. When this step had been taken, the business proceeded more rapidly, and on the 31st of March, 1713, the Treaty of Utrecht was signed.

This famous instrument, which gave Great Britain peace for a generation, was in no way due to the statesmen who actually signed it. Oxford and Bolingbroke were responsible for deceiving the Dutch, and betraying the Catalans. Gibraltar, Newfoundland, Nova Scotia, and Hudson's Bay, the substantial fruits of the great war, were due to the financial capacity of Godolphin, who was dead, and to the military genius of Marlborough, who was in exile. The Tories had opposed the war, and were not entitled to claim any credit for the peace. The banishment of the Pretender, and the security of the Protestant Succession, were no objects of desire with Bolingbroke, who, if he could, would have repealed the Act of Settlement, and enthroned James the Third. He may be allowed to claim, or to share with Oxford, the glory of the Asiento, by which Britain received the exclusive privilege of supplying the Spanish possessions in America with negro slaves. Philip's renunciation of the French Crown, declared by French lawyers, and by the Duke of Saint-Simon, to be invalid in law, would almost certainly have been found worthless in fact, if Louis the Fifteenth had not falsified general expectation by living to inherit his great-grandfather's dominions. Little statesmanship was required to gather the fruits of other men's victories, and to extract from France what she had no power to withhold. The diplomatic instrument itself was complicated and confusing to ordinary minds. "My Lord Oxford's peace," said Wharton profanely, "is like the peace of God; it passes all understanding." Nevertheless the Treaty of Utrecht was popular, and in making it the Ministers gave effect to the will of the people. At the General Election of 1713 they received the approval of the nation, and the Whigs seemed to have no chance of regaining power. Two causes, however, were working silently in their favour. One was the staunch Catholicism of James; the other was the restless ambition of Bolingbroke. A Catholic sovereign of Great Britain was impossible, and the only alternative to James the Third, unless the Electress survived the Queen, was George the First. The House of Hanover was essentially and inevitably Whig. Its title to the throne of Great Britain and Ireland was Parliamentary. Its enemies, believers in divine right, were all Tories. Hanover had taken an active part with the Empire against France in the War of the Spanish Succession. It was Protestant to the core, and commanded the support of all Whigs. While the Whigs were united by adversity, the Tories were divided by prosperity. Some were Hanoverians, others were Jacobites. Tories who would not willingly in set terms acknowledge any one except James Stuart as their lawful sovereign, were willing to recognize a King by Act of Parliament, as their legal ruler, to whom obedience might without prejudice be rendered. Bolingbroke, even after he despaired of inducing the Pretender to abandon the Catholic faith, had his own game to play. His nominal subordination to Oxford galled him, and it was not a solitary grievance. With all his accomplishments, he had a trivial mind, and he was bitterly disappointed to be put off with a viscounty when he expected an earldom. The Portland manuscripts preserve the proofs of his chagrin, which was inflamed by Anne's bestowal of the Garter upon the Earl of Oxford. He who thinks his place unfit for him, said the Marquess of Halifax, will be unfit for his place. So it was with Bolingbroke in 1713. His mind was not really given to foreign affairs, not even to the Treaty of Utrecht. His main purpose was to supersede Lord Oxford, and to become Lord Treasurer himself. For the White Staff, the symbol of power, or at least of patronage, he would have bartered such prejudices as remained to him, and such principles as he possessed. He would gladly have accepted it under James. He would willingly have accepted it under George. He was bent upon receiving it under Anne. He cultivated an alliance with the Tory Highfliers, and even affected to be a High Churchman, believing that persecution of Dissenters would be as popular with the nation as it would be congenial to the Queen. He was a disturbing element in Oxford's cabinet, and in the Tory ranks. So far as he had any settled convictions in politics, he was against Constitutional monarchy, and favourable to personal rule. Few Tories who were not also Jacobites, and perhaps not all who were, would have followed him in abandoning the restrictions placed by the Revolution upon the Crown. Even the Treaty of Utrecht contained unpalatable matter. Little was said or thought at the time about the fishing rights reserved to

France in Newfoundland, which have since given rise to so much trouble. But there were also questions of trade.

Besides the general peace, Bolingbroke had concluded a commercial treaty with France, which gave her the rights of the most favoured nation, providing that no foreign imports should pay a lower duty than the French. In 1713 this was regarded, and with reason, as a long step towards complete freedom of trade. But it was a direct infringement of the Methuen Treaty with Portugal, under which the duty on Portuguese wine must be one-third less than was paid by the wine of France. The Whigs took this point in the House of Commons, and the manufacturers of woollens were so much alarmed for the possible loss of their business with Portugal, if the Methuen Treaty were infringed, that the Bill adopting the convention was finally defeated on the 18th of June. Nor was this the only Whig triumph. Both Houses agreed to address the Queen in favour of removing the Pretender from Lorraine, although she had in fact no control over the Duke of Lorraine, or over her own brother, and nothing happened in consequence of these votes.

Bolingbroke's avowed policy of using his power for the benefit of his friends was adopted in ecclesiastical, as well as in secular, affairs. On the 23rd of March, 1713, the period for which the House of Lords had suspended Sacheverell from preaching, came to an end, and a Tory House of Commons invited this noisy Jacobite to preach before them on the anniversary of the Restoration. The Queen was not unwilling to make him a bishop. But this was felt to be too strong an approval of passive obedience, and Sacheverell had to be content with the Crown living of St. Andrew's, Holborn, which gave him a large share of the notoriety he loved. No one had a more open contempt for Sacheverell than Jonathan Swift, who aspired to a! bishopric at this time. Here, however, Anne put down her foot. The man who had written the Tale of a Tub, though he had prudently abstained from putting his name to it, should not, while she lived, be a bishop either in the Church of England or in the Church of Ireland. It is impossible not to respect the scruples of the Queen. The Tale of a Tub could not have been written by a man who had any spiritual reverence, and that Swift should himself have desired a bishopric is not the least startling feature of his enigmatic disposition. A middle course was found by promoting Dr. Sterne to the Bishopric of Dromore, and appointing Swift to be Dean of St. Patrick's, on the 23rd of April, in Sterne's room. Swift's powerful, irrepressible genius soon made him the greatest man in Ireland, though he derived no happiness from the influence he wielded. He had sold himself to Oxford and Bolingbroke. By dint of always preaching Toryism he had unconsciously become a Tory. But Swift was no Jacobite. He was attached to his Protestant Church as a political institution. Of ministerial intrigues with St. Germains he knew nothing, and it is to his honour that he was never entrusted with the knowledge. Far different was the case of Francis Atterbury, promoted at this time from the Deanery of Christchurch to the Deanery of Westminster and Bishopric of Rochester, then usually combined. Atterbury's High Churchmanship stopped short of Rome, from which it was divided theologically by a thin, impalpable line, and practically by the Pope. But he would certainly have had no objection to a Catholic Sovereign, and there was not a more thorough-going Jacobite in the Church of England than he. His removal from Christchurch was a blessing to the College, which was never at peace during the short period of his headship, and which he would have reduced, if more time had been given him, to the condition of Trinity under Bentley. In the House of Lords, if circumstances had not soon placed him on his own defence, he would have agitated for repealing the Act of Settlement with as much pugnacity, and as little information, as he displayed in arguing for the absurd Letters of Phalaris.

Atterbury's appointment was a declaration of open war against Whigs, Low Churchmen, Dissenters, and Hanoverians. Yet it produced strangely little effect upon the country, when the Parliament of 1710 came under the Triennial Act to be dissolved in the summer of 1713. The peace was so popular that a Government which contained at least one ardent Jacobite received votes from electors who burnt together in effigy the Devil, the Pope, and the Pretender. The Whigs gained a few seats, but not enough to disturb their opponents, or to encourage themselves. The Tories were resolved to make hay while the sun shone. On the 18th of March, 1714, they expelled Richard Steele, Member for Stockbridge, a Whig essayist inferior only to Addison, from the House of Commons for publishing a pamphlet called the Crisis in favour of the Hanoverian succession, which happened to be the law of the land. That succession was altered by death on the 28th of May. The Electress Sophia once said that she would die happy, if she could be described on her coffin as Queen of England. Considering that her son was older than Queen Anne, the Electress may be thought immoderate in her ambition, near as she came to fulfilling it. She died suddenly in her eighty-fourth year, partly, it is thought, from vexation, because Anne, who had no wish for the society of her own heirs, declined to receive in England Sophia's son the Elector, or her grandson the Electoral Prince, who as Duke of Cambridge was entitled to a writ of summons for the House of Lords. Although the Elector had quarrelled with Marlborough, who would not trust him with military secrets in 1708, his Whig leanings were well known, and the English Tories were pulling fast towards the rapids. The nearer they came, the harder they pulled. In the session of 1714 they carried the Schism Act, for which the much abused word incredible seems the most appropriate epithet. By this statute, which was never, as things turned out, enforced. Englishmen were forbidden to act as tutors or school-masters, except in noblemen's families, without conforming to the Church of England. A touch of burlesque is imparted to the infamy of such a law by the ludicrous exception already named, and by the fact that its most strenuous champion was Henry St. John, Viscount Bolingbroke, a nominal Deist, an actual sceptic, scoffer, and rake. After this Act had been passed, and before Parliament had been prorogued, the Government offered a reward, hypocritical so far as Bolingbroke was concerned, and not very sincere on the part of Oxford, for the apprehension of James Stuart upon British soil. It was originally five thousand pounds, but the House of Commons increased it to a hundred thousand. There was no real danger of a Stuart restoration, or the House of Hanover would have been impossible. But at a time when nobody trusted anybody else, when public morality was on much the same level as Thucydides has described in his account of the troubles at Corcyra, effusive outbursts of loyalty to the Act of Settlement were as common as they were false. What really kept the mass of honest Englishmen, not involved in political intrigues, true to the Protestant Succession, was no statute, and no Parliament; it was the memory of James the Second's reign and the history of Mary Tudor's.

On the 9th of July, 1714, the Session drew to a close. Within a few days the quarrel between Oxford and Bolingbroke came to a head. The life of one frail woman, prematurely old, and exhausted by a long series of illnesses, stood between the chiefs of the Tory Ministry and a cataclysm of political ruin. Yet they could find no better occupation than to intrigue against each other. Bolingbroke was the more active plotter of the two, because he had failed to get what he wanted, and was not the head of the Government. He had good reason to know that his plan of restoring James, after the death of Anne, in which his friend Atterbury believed, would be frustrated by James's loyalty to the Catholic faith. He cherished a hope, which must have been faint, of making his peace with the Elector, and meanwhile he was resolved to be the First Minister of Anne. Oxford's incapacity helped him, and so did the growing sottishness which made the Lord Treasurer odious to the Queen. Even Lady Masham, to whom Bolingbroke paid assiduous court in a political sense, had turned against her kinsman, partly because Oxford was out of favour with her mistress, and partly, it is probable, because he had failed to co-operate with her in some scheme of making money at the public expense. The best account of this miserable squabble is to be found in a sombre and mournful letter, written thirteen years after the event by Swift to Oxford's son. Swift had scarcely been installed in his Deanery of St. Patrick's when numerous letters from England implored him to return, and to effect a reconciliation. No one could appeal to the reason better than Swift, so long as he retained his own. But Oxford and Bolingbroke were beyond the reach of argument. Oxford was in an almost chronic state of alcoholic torpor, and Bolingbroke was madly bent upon ousting his rival without delay. "When I returned to England," wrote Swift on the 14th of June, 1737, "I found their quarrels and coldness increased. I laboured to reconcile them as much as I was able. I contrived to bring them to my Lord Masham's, at St. James's. My Lord and Lady Masham left us together. I expostulated with them both but could not find any good consequences. I was to go to Windsor next day with my Lord Treasurer: I pretended business that prevented me, expecting they would come to some agreement. But I followed them to Windsor, where my Lord Bolingbroke told me that my scheme had come to nothing. Things went on at the same rate: they grew more estranged every day. My Lord Treasurer found his credit daily declining. In May 1714 I had my last meeting with them at my Lord Masham's. He left us together, and therefore I spoke very fully to them both; and told them 'I would retire, for I found all was gone.' Lord Bolingbroke whispered me, 'I was in the right.' Your father said, 'All would do well.'"

Swift, who knew better, was powerless, and retired to Berkshire, where he stayed, a strange guest, with a clerical friend. It was on the 27th of July, 1714, that Bolingbroke achieved his momentary triumph in the dismissal of Oxford, after a stormy altercation in the Royal Closet, and a torrent of undignified reproaches from the Queen. Who was to be the new Lord Treasurer? A more utterly insignificant question never presented itself to the mind of man. But to Bolingbroke it was the one thing in all the world that mattered. He did not get the White Staff himself. The disputes which led to Oxford's compulsory retirement had prostrated the Queen, and on the 30th of July she was at death's door. Bolingbroke was no favourite of hers. His irreligion and immorality were not to her mind. With her dying hands she gave the staff to the Duke of Shrewsbury, who was recommended by the Cabinet, with the sulky acquiescence of Bolingbroke, and bade him use it for the good of her people. Shrewsbury, though he played a double part, like so many statesmen of his time, was an active supporter of the Revolution, and of the Exclusion Bill. Whatever he may have been in 1700, or in 1715, when the Whigs had ousted him, he was in 1714 a staunch adherent to the Protestant Succession, and to the House of Hanover. If the Queen had lived, Bolingbroke might have supplanted Shrewsbury, as he supplanted Oxford, and a Jacobite conspiracy might for a time, though not for long, have succeeded. But the Queen's strength was dwindling every hour. She had no wish to live. "Sleep," said Dr. Arbuthnot, "was never more welcome to a weary traveller than death was to her." There is no truth in the legend that she showed remorse for her treatment of her father, or of her brother. "Death is the triumph of the physical," and the appointment of Shrewsbury was Anne's last conscious act, though she survived till the morning of the 1st of August.

Meanwhile there had assembled at Kensington Palace what would now be called a Cabinet. Anne would naturally have been there. But her absence on this occasion, though it portended a change of dynasty, was less notable than the presence of two Whig Peers, the Dukes of Somerset and Argyll. As they were not in office, they had not been summoned. They were, however, Privy Councillors, and they asserted their right to be present at a Committee of the Privy Council. Shrewsbury made them welcome. Bolingbroke did not venture to keep them out. He was a victim of the moral paralysis which habitually assailed him when action was required. The Whigs were at least men, and Argyll in particular was a strong man. They knew their own minds, and made adequate preparations against the danger of a Jacobite rising. When the Queen died, five days after Oxford's removal, the Government was really, though not formally, in Whig hands. Whigs held command of the army and of the navy. The ports were watched. A ship was sent to Holland, where George the First could embark for his new kingdom. Marlborough waited at Ostend for a favourable wind, a Hanoverian by inclination, but prepared for either event. When he did come to England in support of King George, he was too late, and his services were not required. The Whigs of those days were essentially placemen, and their standard of public morality would now be considered deplorably low. Bolingbroke himself was not more greedy of power and patronage than they. But they were also men of action, bold, resolute, determined; unlike the Tories, except Atterbury, who was a bishop, and alone. They understood business, diplomacy, and war. Formal praise would be wasted upon statesmen whose interests coincided with their duty. For the Whigs the Hanoverian dynasty signified a long, an indefinite prospect of honour and emolument. They took the tide at the flood, and it led them on to fortune. There was probably no one whom Bolingbroke, the literary dreamer, hated or despised as he despised and hated the illiterate Walpole. But while Bolingbroke quoted Horace, and wrapped himself in his own virtue, a threadbare suit, Walpole, consolidating his position by all means, good and bad alike, became the first statesman in England, if not in Europe. England passed under the domination of the Whigs with the final breath that left the body of Queen Anne.

As George the First was still in Hanover, a list of Regents had been drawn up before the actual demise of the Crown. Besides seven officers of State who were entitled to places in it, the Archbishop of Canterbury standing first, and the Lord Chancellor second, it included eighteen noblemen, five of whom were Tories. Marlborough and Somers were conspicuous by their absence, praefulgebant quia non visebantur. The Proclamation which actually notified the death of Anne, and the accession of George, was signed by Bolingbroke, and several other Jacobites. When it was read at Westminster, and in the City of London, the loyal cheers were unbroken by a single hiss. That sign of public feeling was reserved for Oxford and Bolingbroke, who in their quarrel with each other had ruined themselves. The Whigs carried everything before them, though Ormond's personal popularity ensured him a' good reception. The sentiments of the people admitted of no doubt. A Protestant sovereign and a tranquil reign were the objects of their desire. The Act of Settlement had the support of public opinion because it saved England from the Pope and the Pretender.

The life of Anne resolves itself at the beginning of her reign into the history of England, of Scotland, and of Europe. The history of Ireland, a mere history of oppression, was illuminated in subsequent years by the savage satire of the great Dean, who withdrew at the death of the Queen to Dublin, and there wreaked his vengeance upon Whigs in particular, and the human race in general. Throughout the mighty drama of the disputed succession and the Spanish war Anne was a dumb character, a lay figure on the stage. Of the four English Queens she is by far the least significant. Even Mary Tudor is redeemed from nonentity by her policy of "thorough" in religious persecution. Anne did her best, in circumstances of peculiar embarrassment, to fulfil her obligations amidst the selfish intriguers who surrounded her. But her task was almost impossible. She laboured for the peace which only came in the last year of her reign, not because she was a prudent sovereign, but because she was a conscientious woman. She gave lavishly to the Church of England. Otherwise she was little more than a bone of contention between ambitious statesmen and plotting favourites. Her one political conviction was that the Whigs were enemies of the Church. In that and some other respects she was curiously like George the Third. If she had been gifted with his cunning and his strength of will, she would have made a push for personal rule. She presided, as we have seen, at her own Cabinets. She assisted, almost as regularly as Charles the Second, at the debates in the House of Lords. She resented the coercion of Godolphin's Whig ministry, and it was by playing upon this resentment that Mrs. Masham acquired the influence which put Harley in the place of Godolphin. When the favourite used, or abused, her ascendency for the second time, and did with Oxford as she had done with his predecessor, the Queen's strength had been exhausted, and the whole fabric of bedchamber intrigue fell to pieces like a house of cards. The Duchess of Burgundy told Catherine de Medicis that a country with a King was governed by women, and a country with a Queen was governed by men. Anne and her female favourites did not, could not govern. The ruling forces of her reign were Marlborough and Godolphin. Her sad life was as inconspicuous as the life of royalty can be. Married to a husband whom she could not respect, seeing all her children die in childhood, watching the gradual dissolution of her ardent friendship for the playmate of her youth, she did find a real friend, if not a disinterested one, in Abigail Masham. Suspicion, the besetting sin of the narrow-minded, haunted Anne's life and increased its gloom. The secret tragedy of her maimed existence and her wasted years may be read in the little coffins at Westminster Abbey, where the bodies of her children are laid.

CHAPTER III: LITERATURE

Before Walpole and the Hanoverians banished literature from public life, men of letters were, almost an estate of the nation. Addison, Pope, Swift, and Bolingbroke were not only united in good fellowship; they were also glad to welcome any man of genius, like Prior, and ready to assist every young author who deserved it. London was then so small a place that nothing good could be published there without the writer becoming, in a short time, familiar to the literary circle of the metropolis. It was not unlike the Augustan age so admirably described by Ben Jonson in Sejanus, although there was no cultivated Caesar. Halifax, Oxford, and Shrewsbury, if the two former were not competent critics, were all three generous patrons, so that, though the spirit of party was at its height, literature united men whom politics divided. There could be no better example of this pleasant freemasonry than the case of William Harrison. Harrison was the son of a country doctor, and became through Addison "governor" or tutor to the Duke of Queensberry's son. Addison also recommended him to Swift as an ingenious composer of Latin verse, and author of some English poems in the Tatler. "A little pretty fellow," Swift called him in writing to Stella, "with a great deal of wit, good sense, and good nature." When Steele gave up the Tatler at the end of 1710, Swift, with great kindness, helped Harrison to carry it on, freely correcting what he frankly described as Harrison's "trash." The enterprise was not successful, and Harrison was quick to spend whatever he earned. But Swift's unaccustomed benevolence was not exhausted. A man, he thought, might fail in literature, and yet succeed in diplomacy. St. John was Secretary of State, and the Peace Conference was about to meet at the Hague. "I was this morning at the Secretary, St. John's," wrote Swift to Stella, on the 15th of March, 1711, "and he has given me for young Harrison the Tatler, the prettiest employment in Europe, Secretary to my Lord Raby, who is to be Ambassador Extraordinary at the Hague, where all the great affairs will be concerted, so we shall lose the Tatler in a fortnight." Harrison came home with the Barrier Treaty at the beginning of 1712, but died of a fever in his twenty-eighth year. Swift's attention to him during his last illness was extraordinary, and he told Stella that no loss had ever grieved him so much. Harrison is not himself an important person, though his Woodstock Park, in Dodsley's collection of poetry, is still read. The interest of his brief career lies in his relation to the older writers who befriended him and provided for him. It was a real confraternity of letters to which Swift introduced Harrison, and even Congreve, in his blindness, was at pains to write for the young man's Tatler. Such things are only possible in a small society, where every denizen of Grub Street knows all the rest. Addison's course, though chequered and disturbed by politics, is a very remarkable instance of literary merit rewarded by public office and honour. But still more striking and more agreeable than the patronage of Halifax or Godolphin was the cordial sympathy with which the masters of the pen regarded each other. There has been nothing quite like it since. There are too many people in the world, especially in London, and competition is too fierce. After the censorship of the Press had ceased, and before Parliamentary reporting had begun, the little group of pamphleteers who could write were more powerful than the Cabinet, and at least as well known.

Ere Queen Anne became sovereign of England, Scotland, and Ireland, the founder of the literary school which illustrates her reign had passed away. John Dryden died in 1700, after predicting that his "cousin Swift," a distant cousin, would never be a poet. Dryden had seen only the crazy Pindarics with which Swift celebrated, in a metre he did not understand, the virtues of Sir William Temple, whom he feared and therefore hated. He did not live to read the masterpieces of satire and observation which make Swift one of the best writers of familiar verse in the English language. Of Alexander Pope, who was twelve years old at his death, Dryden knew nothing at all. Yet it is as certain as any unverified hypothesis can be, that without Dryden there would have been no Pope; and Pope, though most of his best things were written after 1714, was the one really great poet in the reign of Anne. That in his own way he was a great poet few critics would now deny. The extravagant adulation of Byron, whose praise of the dead was usually meant to give pain to the living, and the rise of the Lake School, whom Byron absurdly decried, combined to bring about a temporary eclipse of Pope's fame. But genius is immortal, and the star of Pope has reappeared. One star differeth from another star in glory. It is idle and unprofitable to compare Pope with Wordsworth or with Keats. He had different ideals, and different methods of pursuing them. But in his own line he has never been surpassed, and he represents the spirit which ruled the eighteenth century, until the French Revolution changed the face of the world. Pope has been called classical, partly because he paraphrased Homer and Horace, partly from the perfection of his literary form. Yet he was no great classical scholar, no match for Swift, or for Lady Mary Wortley. The question how much Greek he knew, or whether he knew Greek at all, lies outside the period of Anne. It is enough to say here that a man of Pope's unrivalled cleverness might have written his pretty poem, as Bentley called his Iliad, from Chapman and Dacier, or from a Latin crib. A good Latinist Pope undoubtedly was, slender and fragmentary as his education had been. He was born in the year of the English Revolution, and his parents were Catholics. Taught by four priests in succession, with two private schools interposed between the third and the fourth, he began from a child to read voraciously, and was scarcely out of his childhood when he commenced author. "I lisped in numbers, for the numbers came," he says, imitating a verse of Ovid, whom in many respects he resembled. Pope's religion, or the religion of his father and mother, shut him out from the public schools, the universities, the legislature, the bar, and every kind of political, military, or municipal office. But for such things he had no aptitude and no inclination. His weapon was the pen, and the success with which he wielded it is embalmed in his own famous couplet —

"Yes, I am proud, and justly proud, to see

Men not afraid of God afraid of me."

His compliments are among the most exquisite ever paid in verse. His invective was so tremendous that the least susceptible shrank from it in fear. The disabilities imposed on him by his hereditary faith he never attempted to remove. He was no more a real Catholic than Bolingbroke was a real Protestant. He was simply a Deist, whose genuine convictions are expressed in the Universal Prayer. If he adhered to the Church of his parents, the reason may be found in that devotion to his mother which is the most amiable feature in a strange, crooked, sidelong character. Injuries received in babyhood produced a physical weakness and deformity to which his moral perversity and falsehood may perhaps be traced. Yet, addicted as he was to a gallantry of the most prurient sort, he seems to have been really fond of Martha Blount, and his friendship for Swift was undoubtedly sincere. Although his treatment of Addison and of Lady Mary Wortley is inexcusable, his love of impish mystification is a peccadillo, and Pope was nothing like the monster of incredible iniquity that he appeared to Whitwell Elwin.

Pope took Addison's early advice to remember that his genius was national, and though he called himself a Whig, kept out of political controversy altogether. He was a man of letters pure and simple, with an added taste for good company, and an especial appreciation of the fairer sex. His masters in literature were Horace, Spenser, Dryden, and Boileau. The majesty of Dryden 's verse was beyond him, for he had no dignity of mind. But he learnt rhythm from Spenser and Dryden, as he learnt criticism from Horace and Boileau. The original part of him was his style; inimitable for neatness, terseness, and point. The part that belonged to his age, and is therefore most to the purpose here, was his sceptical, mocking spirit; his exaltation of common sense; his acceptance of Shaftesbury's canon that ridicule is the test of truth. In these things he resembled Voltaire. Easily as rhymes came to Pope, he polished them to the last degree before they saw the light. His Pastorals, imitated from Virgil's Eclogues, and published in 1709, were by his own account the poems on which he spent most care, and the Messiah, a modern setting of the Pollio, was always his favourite. Whatever else may be thought of these Pastorals, they are copies taken from copies, for Virgil followed, and almost translated, Theocritus. And although the best Greek literature will bear a good deal of watering down, even Theocritus at two removes bears a perilous resemblance to salt without its savour. At twenty-one Pope was a mere bookworm, and his full powers slumbered until he had become thoroughly well acquainted with human nature. The best thing the Pastorals did for him was that they introduced him to Halifax and Congreve. The Essay on Criticism, which came out two years later, in 1711, was written, as we learn from Spence's Anecdotes, "very fast." Here Pope was familiar with his subject, having studied Horace's Art of Poetry as an adept, and thoroughly understood the Roman critic's meaning. The Ars Poetica was not written for beginners, and is quite unintelligible to schoolboys. It is the familiar epistle of a highly cultivated gentleman to correspondents who can take hints without explanations, and can fill up gaps in the sense for themselves. It can never be of any use to readers who try to interpret the suggestive, half-inquiring lines as though they were the finished and formal treatise of an academic professor. Pope did not apprehend Horace as the Pisos apprehended him. But he was quite clever enough to see what sort of thing he was copying, to pick out the salient points, and to leave the difficulties alone. "Horace's Art of Poetry" he said to Spence, "was probably only fragments of what he designed; it wants the regularity that flows from the following a plan; and there are several passages in it that are hints only of a larger design." When Johnson paraphrased Juvenal, he glowed with the feeling of his author. When Pope paraphrased Horace, he was conscious of the excellent opportunities given him by the Latin for the development of his own peculiar talents. Few poets have achieved earlier fame. William Congreve, who admired his Pastorals, was then at the summit of his own renown. Congreve's brilliant comedies had all been produced in the late reign before he was thirty. His one tragedy, The Mourning Bride, so extravagantly praised by Johnson, had succeeded beyond its deserts. Godolphin had provided for him by a Commissionership of Licenses, which enabled him to live in comfort, to set up for a man of fashion, and to pose as an arbiter of taste. Lord Halifax, whose steadfast Whiggery excluded him from office during the reign of Anne, affected the airs of a literary critic without much right to assume them. He was, however, a generous patron of letters, and though Pope derived no material assistance from him, he owed to Halifax his friendship with Addison, and to Addison his friendship with Swift. The relations between Pope and Addison were not altogether satisfactory. But no one ever had a better friend than Pope had in Addison, or than Swift had in Pope.

The Essay on Criticism received warm and due praise from the Spectator, of which the first number appeared on the 1st of March, 1711. It was followed in 1714 by Windsor Forest and the Rape of the Lock. Windsor Forest, an academic exercise, destitute of reality and nature, had the honour to be praised by Wordsworth. Otherwise it possesses little interest now, except to show how Pope assimilated the metre of Dryden. The Rape of the Lock, on the other hand, was a new thing in English poetry, and is a perfect thing of its kind. Founded on the simple fact that Lord Petre, in the fervour of his adoration, cut off a tress of Miss Belle Termor's hair, and designed at first merely to mitigate the heinousness of that offence, it afterwards became, by the introduction of the sylphs as part of the machinery, a singular example of poetry improved by the preternatural. The powers of the air, good-natured spirits, are martialled by Pope with such grace and skill that a trumpery incident of a frivolous amour becomes quite romantic, and almost sublime. Addison incurred Pope's undying resentment by begging him not to touch the original version, in which there were no sylphs. But that most amiable of men would have been the first to acknowledge that his advice was bad, and that Pope had done what any judicious critic would have told him he could not do. Pope's Catholic training may have suggested to him the idea of "metaphysical aid." No one less prodigiously clever could have invoked it in such a cause without incurring the slightest touch of ridicule. The result, charming as it is to-day, was even more appropriate to the age of Anne. It was an age of fops and beaux, of wigs and swords, of love-making rather ostentatious than clandestine, of masks and dominos, duels and dice. London society was quite small enough to know all about Miss Fermor, and Lord Petre, and Sir George Brown, who figured as Pope's "Sir Plume," and did not like being made to talk nonsense all the time; "Sir Plume of amber snuff-box justly vain, and the nice conduct of a clouded cane." The reading public, however, were of a different opinion from Sir George Brown's. Pope was not really more moral than Congreve, perhaps less. But he had written a poem which was like a proper Love for Love, a prim Way of the World, and he seemed to have taken from the devil some of his best tunes. Congreve was guilty of an anachronism, which laid him open to the unsparing lash of Jeremy Collier. He had transferred to the Revolution the morality of the Restoration, when all the world, especially Dryden, was young. The Court of Anne was strictly decorous; and if the whole of the town was not quite so correct as the Court, the parade of vice had ceased to be popular. When Pope was writing only to please himself, as in his version of Horace's second satire, which has never been published since 1738, he could be far more licentious than Dryden or Congreve. But as a rule he exercised restraint, and conformed to a public taste which was neither dissolute nor Puritanical.

Pope did not begin to write, or at least to publish, until the martial ardour excited by Marlborough's campaigns had subsided. He is emphatically the poet of peace and pleasure, "youth at the prow and pleasure at the helm." His mastery of the vernacular gave him a wider popularity than he could have acquired by his grace of style alone, and no English poet except Shakespeare, not even Milton, is so full of passages which have become stock quotations. Although the heroic metre, in which his thoughts, not very profound thoughts, seemed naturally to clothe themselves, has become nearly obsolete, and the secret of his epigrammatic verse has vanished, the attraction of Pope is indestructible with all who have any sense of literary form. If any one will seriously try to improve upon the way in which Pope has expressed his meaning, he will get a more vivid idea of what expression is than by the study of a hundred manuals. The age of Anne was not altogether superficial. It was the age of Newton, of

Berkeley, of Bentley, and of Swift. But its religion and its philosophy, though quite genuine, were not deep. The unbridled license of the Restoration had sprung in part from the meddlesome strictness of the Commonwealth.

With the Revolution began the reign of reason in politics, in morals, and in faith. The ponderous Theism, or Pantheism, of Toland and his school was regarded as a bore. When Swift sneered at "that quality of their voluminous writings which the poverty of the English language compels me to call their style," he made a palpable hit. He would have been the last to depreciate the style of Pope, which, in simplicity and directness, was not unlike his own. Although Pope was not a member of the dominant Church, although he nominally adhered to a small and persecuted communion of disfranchised Englishmen, he hit the lay public between wind and water. Collier had too much religion for them. Shaftesbury had too little. Berkeley was over their heads. Swift frightened them. Pope was every man's poet, the poet of the golden mean, who had true wit because he said what everybody thought, and nobody else could say so well.

Yet in the literature of Anne there was a mightier than Pope. Pope in his most ambitious speculations never went much below the surface. His vein was thin. His mine was shallow. Carlyle loved to tell the story of a Scottish miner, who was asked how far down he had been in the course of his work, and replied that he had heard the devil boasting, or in English coughing. Swift seemed often to hear the sound. He was cursed with a lurid insight into evil, with an eye which pierced the trappings of conventionalism and saw the hypocrisy involved in all civilized behaviour. True goodness he did not see; or, if he saw it, he did not care to dwell upon it. He was that rarest of God's creatures, a misanthrope, to whom the degradation of humanity was a real joy. That the relations of the sexes were the same in men and women as in other animals, was a revolting paradox on which he loved to dwell. All pretence of sanctity, or even of religion, apart from a cold, dry, legal orthodoxy, to be enforced by the secular arm, was to him dishonest affectation. He said openly in talk, and implied in his own ghastly epitaph on himself, that his sermons were political pamphlets. He seldom in all his various writings appeals to a lofty motive, or shows any enthusiasm for a great deed. His chief friends, such as Pope, Harley, and St. John, had neither religion nor virtue. His love of filth amounted to a mania. On the other hand, in a drunken age he was strictly sober, and he was quite capable of disinterested kindness to the few people he really liked. His nature was warped. Capable of inspiring, but incapable of returning, passion, he broke the hearts of two women by his coldness, and the death of Vanessa, Hester Van Homrigh, affected him no more than the death of a dog. Of Stella, Esther Johnson, he was truly fond. But his fondness was not the love of a man for a woman; if it ended in some mysterious, clandestine marriage, of which there is no positive evidence, the marriage was not a real union; and though he was the absorbing interest of her existence, he made her in the end almost as miserable as he made himself. He hated Ireland, where he had to live; he hated the human race; he hated life itself. On his birthday, the day on which, in his own elegant phrase, he was "dropped" on the wrong side of the Irish Channel, he always read the fearful chapter in which Job "opened his mouth, and cursed his day." He was marked from his birth with the stamp of misery and genius. His final catastrophe, the failure of his intellect, belongs to a later period than the period of this book. Till his appointment to the Deanery of St. Patrick's in 1713, and long afterwards, his mind was almost miraculously acute. His humour is not of the deepest kind, because it lacks reverence. Rabelais, his favourite author, hating monks and monkery, revelling in audacious animalism, despising the ceremonies of the Catholic Church, never lost his faith in knowledge or in God. Although Swift is traditionally said to have spent much time at his Deanery in private devotion, his published works show very little religion of any kind. What they do show is an almost inexhaustible storehouse of ludicrous images, a power of murderous satire that no controversialist has ever surpassed, a diamond sense that cut through sophistry like a knife, and a pellucid simplicity of statement that makes the most difficult question easy to the plainest mind. It is possible, of course, to disagree with Swift. It is impossible to misunderstand him.

Swift's early years were hard, and he took them hardly. His father died before he was born, and he never cared for his mother, nor she for him. After leaving Trinity College, Dublin, where he attained no distinction, he became a private secretary to his kinsman, Sir William Temple, at Moor Park, in Surrey, took holy orders, which were not holy in his case, was presented with the small benefice of Laracor, near Dublin, and, residence not being required, came back to Moor Park, where he made up for his idleness at Trinity by a course of steady reading, which made him a sound classical scholar. There he became acquainted with Esther Johnson, another of Temple's poor relations, and there he was goaded by Temple's patronage into that attitude of aggressive hostility against mankind which, as he had a tongue like a razor, procured for him the homage of terror. There can be no doubt that Swift, who was not otherwise clerical, took advantage of his cloth to scatter insults which would have cost a layman many duels, and possibly his life. Women no less than men were the victims of his fury, especially if their social rank was high, for he could not see that to insult a Duchess was simply to insult a woman. His first publication of any importance was evoked by a foolish dispute about the respective merits of ancient and modern writers. Swift's Battle of the Books, an excellent piece of English, has not many other merits, being chiefly designed to cover the deficiencies of his patron, Sir William Temple, who was well qualified to write in defence of the moderns, because he did not know a word of Greek. But Swift's great contribution to literature in the reign of Queen Anne was the Tale of a Tub. It is useless to call in question the merits of a book which critic follows critic in pronouncing to be among the glories of English literature. I will only ask, without answering, how many people read it now. Swift's ostensible object in the Tale of a Tub is to prove that the established Church of England and Ireland, of which he was an ordained minister, is superior to Romanism on the one hand, and to Calvinism on the other. Both Catholics and Protestant Dissenters are adroitly contrived to look exceedingly contemptible and ridiculous. The Church of England, on the other hand, is represented, much less adroitly, to have made the best of a bad job, and to be the only religious communion with which a man of sense may in reason connect himself. If there was one person who held the views which the Tale of a Tub professes to inculcate, that person was Queen Anne. Yet the Queen said, and insisted, that the man who wrote that profane ribaldry should never be a bishop. On a point of this kind one can only express one's own opinion, and I agree with the Queen. I do not believe that any one would have written the Tale of a Tub who had any reverence for Christianity, for religion, or for the Church as a divine institution. Swift never committed himself to a direct statement of disbelief in revelation, in the Bible, or in Christ; but a long course of silence, varied by profane jests at the expense of every other religious body except the jester's own, has a cumulative effect, and leaves upon the mind of an impartial reader a conviction that Swift was far less spiritually minded than the sectaries, or even the Deists, he denounced. The literary merits of the Tale of a Tub are a different question. There is a popular legend that when Swift's intellect was decaying, he took up the Tale and exclaimed, "What a genius I had when I wrote that book." If he had written nothing else, would he now be considered a man of genius at all? The story of the will, and of its interpretation by the three brothers, though exquisitely droll in itself, does not correspond with any historic facts. The brother who represents the Church of England, Martin by name, is no more logical and consistent, though he may be less extravagant, than Peter or Jack. Catholics are treated as if they were not Christians at all, and everything worthy of respect or admiration in their Church is studiously ignored. Nonconformists are to Swift hypocrites of the most loathsome kind, consciously dishonest, and habitually profane. The religious, and even the respectable, part of the community, said that this parson was a jack pudding, to whom all forms of faith were food for flouts and jeers. Even the style is very inferior to what the style of Swift afterwards became, and the whole treatise is unworthy to be mentioned in the same breath with his priceless, incomparable satire on the inconveniences which might result from the immediate abolition of Christianity by law.

Swift's poetry, or rather verse, belongs for the most part to the Georgian era, when he had done with ambition, and with England. His predecessor, Matthew Prior, though inferior to him in humour, far excelled him in beauty of expression, and was endowed with a poetical imagination which Swift wholly lacked. In sheer intellectual power Prior was no match for the great Dean. But if he had never written a line, the man who really negotiated the Treaty of Utrecht would be an important person; and Prior's poems would have made a mere denizen of Grub Street justly famous. He had not Swift's perfect rhythm, and therefore he has been less directly imitated. Cowper, for instance, in the eighteenth century, and Praed in the nineteenth, owed more to Swift than to him. Prior's metre sometimes halts, and his grammar is not always faultless. But the graceful lines beginning "Dear Cloe, how blubbered is that pretty face," quite original, though suggested by Horace, are entirely beyond Swift's range of fancy, and Prior, though often indiscreet, is never disgusting. Educated at Westminster and Cambridge, he knew the classics, if not like a scholar, at least like a gentleman, and they furnished him with many themes for his muse. We need not inquire now-a-days who Prior's Cloe was, or whether he was nice in his amours. His age was not ashamed of sexual passion, and he was a child of his age. He could, however, write in a very different strain, as in his lines to Lady Margaret Holles-Harley, "My noble, lovely little Peggy."

Swift sometimes rose to heights, and often descended to depths, where his readers could not follow him. Prior gave them what they wanted, and though he wrote perhaps too often for the boudoir and the alcove, he charmed their senses without shocking their tastes.

The typical prose of Queen Anne's reign is the prose of Addison and Steele in the Spectator. Although Addison wrote some of the finest hymns in the English language, such as "The spacious firmament on high," and "How are thy servants blest O Lord," together with a drama called Cato, from which quotations are still sometimes made, he is chiefly known to posterity as the painter of Sir Roger de Coverley. Addison's scholarship, as Macaulay points out, was almost confined to the Roman poets, whom at Charterhouse and Oxford he reproduced with wonderful skill. He travelled in Italy, then an unusual feat, and everything he saw there brought to his mind either Latin hexameters, or Latin elegiacs, or Latin lyrics. It was in English verse, as we have seen, that he celebrated Blenheim. But it was in English prose that he made his ineffaceable mark. The shallowest observers of English politics find the party system the easiest thing to abuse. It had not made much progress in the reign of Anne, and the manifestations of it in her last four years are seldom edifying. But one of the debts that literature owes it is the production of the Spectator, founded as a successor to Steele's Tatler, and a counterblast to Swift's Examiner. Swift always wrote anonymously, save when he recommended Lord Oxford, in a rather stilted pamphlet, to found an English Academy of Letters, which would soon have died of ridicule. Addison published his Remarks on Italy and his Dialogues on Medals in his own name. For the Tatler and the Spectator, as afterwards for the Guardian, he wrote without a signature. The Spectator, which lasted in its original shape for about a year and a half, contains his three great characters of Sir Roger de Coverley, Sir Andrew Freeport, and Will Honeycomb, representing the Tory Squire, the Whig fund-holder, and the man about town. The tale is of the slightest. The persons are finished and typical portraits, which hold the mirror up to nature. Addison, assisted in the Spectator by Steele, who had a true and individual genius of his own, was qualified by nature and art to be instructive and at the same time amusing, to read moral lessons in perfect taste without ever becoming a bore. He was throughout his short life a consistent Whig, and yet even Queen Anne could not accuse him of being an enemy to the Church. He was sincerely religious, without a trace of fanaticism; he had a kind heart and a generous temper; his wit was so gentle that when it is keenest it never wounds; and his style is exactly the mode in which an educated gentleman would write to his friends. Very rarely, as in the Vision of Mirza, he rose higher than that, and showed that the deeper mysteries of existence were not beyond his ken. As a rule he gave the cultivated society of his time useful and delicate hints concerning religion, politics, manners, literature, drama, and art. He became the arbiter elegantiarum, the fashionable dictator of an age when fashion had nothing to do with wealth or luxury, but was identified with breeding and behaviour. If Addison had not been rather too fond of wine, he would have had no faults at all; and if hc had preached a rigid sobriety, he would have preached to deaf ears. He did succeed in persuading an age which remembered the Plays of Congreve that vice was dull, dyspeptic, and ill bred. He made the Protestant Succession "the thing," and insinuated without obtruding, a case for the unpopular House of Hanover. Above all, he did what Swift's savage satire could not do. He showed how foolish and how unmannerly it was to laugh at the Christian religion, upon which civilization depended.

Hardly less celebrated as an essayist than Addison, and scarcely less deserving of celebrity, was his friend and coadjutor Richard Steele, also a Charterhouse boy, and also an Oxford man, his college being Merton. Steele's early career was spent in the army, and he had incurred some ridicule by publishing, so far back as 1701, his Christian Hero; for there can be no doubt that, in Johnson's charitable language, he practised the lighter vices. Like Addison, he was a Whig, and his party spirit was much less temperate than his friend's. But he was essentially a good-natured man, easy and tolerant whenever he was not engaged in defending Whigs and attacking Tories. We have seen how Steele excited the wrath of his political opponents by his pamphlet on the crisis in 1713, and how he paid the penalty in a most unjust expulsion from the House of Commons. But politics played a very small part in the Tatler, or in the Spectator, both of which he founded and carried on with Addison's help. The sharp contrast which Thackeray draws between the two men, professing, and proving, that Steele can be imitated, while asserting that Addison is inimitable, will not hold. Subsequent critics have been too much in the habit of blindly following Johnson, who laid down in his dictatorial way the proposition, that the art of writing prose could only be learnt by studying Addison. Johnson himself followed Quintilian on Cicero. But such dogmatism is misleading. Dryden is a better model than Addison, and Swift wrote simpler English than either. Moreover, Steele and Addison are so much alike that it is not always possible to distinguish their work in the Spectator, and Steele was the actual creator, though not the complete author, of Sir Roger de Coverley. That Addison was always above Steele is an exaggeration. His general level is perhaps higher, and certainly more correct. His humour is far more subtle and delicate. On the other hand, he had no enthusiasm, and could not have depicted the lady whom it was a liberal education to love. Nor has he, with all his grace and sympathy, written anything like Steele's reminiscences of his brief military course, which it may be well here to set down:

"Who can have lived in an army, and in a serious hour reflect upon the many gay and agreeable men that might long have flourished in the arts of peace, and not join with the imprecations of the fatherless and widow on the tyrant to whose ambition they fell sacrifices? But gallant men who are cut off by the sword move rather our veneration than our pity; and we gather relief enough from their own contempt of death to make it no evil which was approached with so much cheerfulness, and attended with so much honour."

To learn an essay of Addison's or of Steele's by heart, would be a far more profitable occupation than to show why one was better or worse than the other.

During the whole of Queen Anne's reign, Isaac Watts was a Nonconformist minister in London, a man of liberal mind, author of many noble hymns, and of some bad Court odes. He is said to have written six hundred hymns in all. Two at least are universally popular and superlatively good. "Jesus shall reign where'er the sun," has the more personal interest because Watts himself inclined to Arianism. But his masterpiece, perhaps the finest hymn in the English language, first published in 1707, is "O God, our help in ages past." It is of course a paraphrase of the ninetieth psalm, that sublime expression of pure theism. Whereas, however, most metrical versions of the psalms are faint and feeble efforts, almost parodies, this stands out as superior in dignity, majesty, and beauty, even to the splendid translation from the Vulgate in the Book of Common Prayer.

If Isaac Watts, educated, and very well educated, at Stoke Newington, was the glory of the free churches, or the churches which ought to have been free, the glory of the Established Church was not Swift, who should never have been a clergyman at all, but Berkeley. George Berkeley, the greatest philosopher ever produced by Trinity College, Dublin, came to England in 1713, where he was welcomed by the circle of Pope, Swift, Addison, and Steele. He had already published his New Theory of Vision, his Treatise Concerning Human Knowledge, and his Dialogues between Hylas and Philonous, that is to say, between a materialist and a spiritualist in the proper sense of those terms. Berkeley was one of the few Greek scholars in any university at that time, and no English writer has come nearer to the perfection of Plato in the art of philosophical dialectic. The assailants of Christianity, Shaftesbury and Mandeville, at whom he more particularly aimed his shafts, were not formidable in themselves. Berkeley's own philosophy has long survived the controversies of his own day, and become the permanent heritage of speculative mankind. He was subject to much vulgar ridicule because he denied, or at all events doubted, the reality of the external world, and "coxcombs vanquished Berkeley with a grin," as they have continued to do ever since. He who denied that the world was manifest to our senses would of course be a lunatic. But appearance is not reality, and things are not what they seem. Of those who maintained, like Tyndall in our own day, that matter alone existed, Berkeley inquired how they knew that matter existed at all. He did not foresee that Hume would carry the investigation a step further, and ask what proof there was for the existence of mind, to which perhaps the best answer is, that we can put the question. Berkeley had to deal with materialism, in his time a not unfashionable creed, and he dealt it a blow from which it has never recovered. His Irish bishopric belongs to the future, when the Irish Church was past saving. In Queen Anne's reign he was only a clergyman. But among all the wits of that reign there were few wittier, and none more wise than he.

Shaftesbury, on the other hand, the third Earl, and Bernard Mandeville, whom Berkeley honoured with a refutation, are almost entirely forgotten. Shaftesbury was a disciple of Pierre Bayle, but he had neither the depth nor the eloquence of that great writer. His Characteristics, published in 1711, would have attracted little notice if they had not been written by a person of quality. Thomas Hill Green, the Oxford Hegelian, calls them a "thin and stilted rhapsody." They had the temporary effect of making smart young gentlemen think that, if ridicule were indeed the test of truth, they could laugh England's Christianity, as Cervantes had laughed Spain's chivalry, away. They also made "the moral sense" a fashionable phrase in circles where there was little sense and less morality. But they did not contribute much to the advancement of any theory, or the formation of any school. Mandeville, a native of Holland, and a doctor of Leyden, had no such ambition. He believed as fully as Swift in the vileness of human nature, and he inculcated the utility of vice, in his Fable of the Bees, with a frankness never surpassed. Socrates would have enjoyed an argument with Mandeville, whose thesis that private vices are public benefits is quite in the vein of Polus or Thrasymachus. At the time of the Restoration, when Hudibras was popular, Mandeville might have had the honour of being taken to church by Charles the Second. But he came too late, except for Berkeley, and otherwise he only amused the curious. From 1660 to 1685 vice, public and private, had had full swing. It was glorified after the Revolution with exquisite taste, in the Comedies of Congreve, which still kept the stage, Jeremy Collier notwithstanding. The English people, however, did not want to make a theory of it. Most of them would rather be hypocrites than pay no homage to virtue at all.

The principal dramatist of Queen Anne's reign was Vanbrugh, the architect of Blenheim, and of Castle Howard. George Farquhar, who died before he was thirty, brought out in 1707 his best play, The Beau's Stratagem, and Mrs. Centlivre, wife of the Queen's cook, herself an actress, wrote eighteen, which have entirely perished, except one phrase, "the real Simon Pure." Professor Saintsbury has acutely observed that a moral improvement, perhaps due to the strictures of Jeremy Collier, may be traced in the plays of this reign. They turn indeed, like Dryden's and Congreve's, upon intrigue and gallantry. But the intrigue is commonly unsuccessful, and the gallantry therefore wasted. This is perhaps not very much for the non-juring parson to have accomplished by all the eloquence which he bestowed upon his Short View of the Immorality and Profaneness of the English Stage. But it is better than nothing, and every little helps. Vanbrugh was in the habit, a habit which did not die with him, of adapting plays from the French, and his most successful piece. The Confederacy, was derived from Dancourt's Bourgeoises a la Mode. There is little to be said for the morality of such plays as the Confederacy, and the good Queen always declined to patronise the stage in any way. Her standard of decorum was high, not to say prudish, and for literature, which Vanbrugh's dramas certainly are, she did not care at all. Shakespeare was not then in vogue, and no one ventured to bring him on the stage, until Colley Cibber had rewritten him. Anne had herself, at the instigation of Charles the Second, been taught the management of her musical voice by an actress, Mrs. Barry, who did not retire till 1710, when she and Mrs. Bracegirdle, the friend of Congreve, were both eclipsed by the rising star of Mrs. Oldfield. The chief actor was Colley Cibber, who may be said to have bridged the period between Betterton and Garrick. No one claimed for the stage, in Queen Anne's time, that it was a virtuous profession, or expected actors and actresses to be bound by the principles of average decorum. Their principle was that those who live to please must please to live. That the stage had a mission, or any other object than the amusement of the public, would have been regarded as a priggish paradox. It was not meant for puritans, parsons, or young ladies, nor was it recruited from the upper and middle ranks of society. All that can be said for it is that actors like Barton Booth, whom even Queen Anne condescended to notice, or Robert Wilks, or Thomas Doggett, founder of the Waterman's badge, knew their business, and that the profession was appreciably less immoral than it had been in the days of the Merry Monarch.

Music, for which the Queen was as enthusiastic as she could be for anything, except the Church, included one illustrious name. George Frederick Handel, a native of Saxony, born in 1685, came to England in 1710, and never left this country after 1712, when he broke his contract with the Elector of Hanover to remain here, so that he is not unfairly reckoned among English composers. Most of his operas, and his mighty oratorios, were produced under Hanoverian auspices. But his Rinaldo, his Pastor Fido, and his Utrecht Te Deum, glorified the reign of Anne. Although he studied in Italy, and was the pupil of Scarlatti, his native force and his inexhaustible genius rank him with the great original composers of all time. No such music had been heard in England before; and Swift's ignorant contempt of it, displayed in his popular couplet about Tweedledum and Tweedledee, Handel and Buononcini, is an example which shows how little the countrymen of Milton knew about the instrumental orchestra, familiar as they were with singing, and with the peal of the anthem from cathedral choirs. Vanbrugh introduced opera from Italy, bringing over Nicolini and Santini to the playhouse in the Haymarket, which he built himself. But it failed for want of subscribers, and Vanbrugh was out of pocket by the transaction.

The painting, like the music, of the early eighteenth century came from Germany. Sir Godfrey Kneller's real name was Gottfried Kniller, and he was born at Lubeck. He was nearly thirty when he first arrived in England, and more than thirty when he began his courtier's career by executing a portrait of Charles the Second. Among his subsequent victims, who included ten reigning sovereigns, were Louis the Fourteenth, William the Third, Peter the Great, and of course Queen Anne herself. Few persons of importance in England escaped being painted by Kneller when the eighteenth century was young. The features of his men are disguised by their full bottomed wigs, and he had too much task-work for the complete development of his powers. His treatment of Marlborough is conventional. But his portrait of the Duchess, now at Windsor, is painted with wonderful verve, and helps one to realize, as nothing else does, the empire she exercised over the greatest man of her time. Kneller's Sarah shows what he might have done if he had been left to himself, and not confined in gilded chains. For Marlborough we must go to the bust in the British Museum, or to the print, also at Windsor, which depicts him as a brilliant young ensign in the French Guard.

The age of Anne has been called Augustan, and was certainly, except the latter part of Elizabeth's reign, the greatest literary age in the history of England. Of its science there is not much to be said. Although Newton's Optics appeared in 1704, his marvellous series of discoveries had been made before the Revolution; he retired from the representation of his University in Parliament at the death of William; and his later years were spent in furthering the cause of Liberal theology. Richard Bentley, as eminent in scholarship as Sir Isaac Newton was in science, had also established his reputation before the close of the seventeenth century, by his unrivalled treatise on the forged letters of Phalaris, and had settled down as Master of Trinity to that chronic struggle with his Fellows which mainly occupied his last forty years. He was too far above his contemporaries in classical scholarship for them to judge him accurately, or at all. But it is unnecessary for arriving at a critical estimate of his powers to follow, or even to approach, the case of Phalaris. Bentley's short letter on a very bad book, Joshua Barnes's edition of Homer, which will be found in Bishop Monk's biography, is a perfect example of philological criticism at its highest and best. It is curious that Richard Bentley and Lewis Theobald, the first two scholars and critics of their age, were both included in the Dunciad by Alexander Pope, who knew, in the true sense of knowledge, nothing at all. No commentator on Shakespeare's text can be compared with Theobald, who restored the true reading, "babbled o' green fields," to Mrs. Quickly's account of Falstaff's death in Henry the Fifth. No edition of Shakespeare, not even Johnson's, is so utterly worthless as

Pope's. It may seem paradoxical to call the age of Newton and Bentley shallow. Nor must we forget that Edmund Halley, of St. Paul's and Queen's College, Oxford, Newton's worthy coadjutor, predicted in 1705 that the comet of 1682 would return in 1758, as after his own death it punctually did. Few discoveries in scholarship can be set above Bentley's restoration of the lost digamma to the metre of Homer, as explained by him with his habitual lucidity in 1713.

The days of newspapers half knowing everything, from the cedar to the hyssop, had not begun, though the Daily Courant was founded, by way of experiment, in 1702. And yet the age as a whole was shallow, spite of lonely thinkers, like Newton, and obscure students, like Theobald. Lady Mary Pierrepont, afterwards Wortley, and finally Wortley-Montagu, who made herself a sound classical scholar while other girls flirted and danced, is a rare exception which proves that the rule was the other way. The Tatler and the Spectator represented, even in cultivated society, the utmost stretch of learning that could be expected from a lady, or even from a gentleman. The whole controversy about ancient and modern writers, which produced Swift's agreeable trifle, The Battle of the Books, was conducted by men none of whom understood both sides of the question, while few of them understood either. Most of them thought that Atterbury had scored a brilliant triumph over Bentley, whose position he could not appreciate, and whose proofs he was incapable of correcting. Swift was justly severe upon the superficial Deism of Collins and Toland. But Swift's own philosophy was of the flimsiest; he did not even see what Berkeley meant; nor did Samuel Clarke's Lectures on the Being and Attributes of God advance the science of theology. Indeed the chief point about these Boyle lectures delivered by Clarke is that they were criticized in 1713 by Joseph Butler, the future bishop, then a young Presbyterian of twenty-one, who had not yet conformed to the Church of England, or gone up to Oxford. The struggle between the Whig bishops in the Upper House of Convocation, and the Tory parsons in the Lower, which led to a joint pronouncement that the Church was not in peril, were infinitely trivial. Swift saw wider and deeper than most of his contemporaries. But even he did not see deep or wide, except into the faults and follies of human nature. The spirit of the time was embodied in Pope, who packed up neat moral maxims in small handy parcels. That he performed his task with consummate dexterity does not alter the nature of it. The world went very well then for the upper ranks of society, and the others did not count. Democracy was considered equivalent to anarchy, and therefore the proper place for a democrat was held to be a lunatic asylum or a gaol. Religion was not meant to curtail the enjoyments of the rich, but to keep the poor in their places, and to prevent the lower orders from rising above their station in life.

Men of letters, with a very few exceptions, depended upon the patronage of the wealthy, who were called the great. Offices of emolument, if not of honour, were bestowed upon masters of the pen on condition that they devoted it to the service of their employers.

That the public was the best patron could hardly be perceived in the absence of copyright, and there was no copyright in published matter at common law. In 1710 the first Copyright Act was passed, and a very mild statute it proved to be. All copies of printed books were vested in their authors, with a power of sale, for the brief period of fourteen years, provided that the book was registered at Stationers' Hall, and deposited with certain public libraries in Great Britain, of which the British Museum was the chief. The act did not apply to Ireland, where books printed in England or Scotland could be freely pirated, if any one were found to buy them. So the law remained more than a hundred and thirty years. Inadequate as was the protection it afforded to authors, it recognized a great principle, and, except the Act of Union with Scotland, this was the most important statute passed in the reign of Anne. The idea that property can consist of ideas had been foreign to the law of England. By way of encouraging literature, it was held that if a man wished to remain owner of his thoughts, he must keep them to himself, and that if he wanted to derive any advantage from his written compositions, he must not publish them. Letters were sacred, and could not be printed without the consent of the writer. Books were profane, and anybody could make what use he pleased of them. It was a good beginning for the age of reason, as the eighteenth century has been called, to destroy this false antithesis, and to bring the common law for once into harmony with common sense.

Common sense is indeed the chief characteristic of literature in Queen Anne's reign. The poetry of Pope, and the prose of Swift, are almost perfect in form. Even Swift's familiar verse, which can scarcely be called poetry, is punctiliously and invariably correct. But until he wrote Gulliver's Travels, which belongs to a later period. Swift showed very little imagination, and it is satire, not fancy, which inspired that savage immortal book. Cadenus and Vanessa, which purports to be a love-poem, is as destitute of poetry as of love. Prior's amatory verses are simple, direct, and human enough for the most exacting of literary naturalists. But they have no air and fire, such as redeem the songs of the seventeenth century from the charge of mere licentiousness. There are few ideas in Pope, consummate artist as he was, which could not be equally well expressed in prose; and when he came to English Horace, though no other writer has Englished Horace so well, it is the sermo pedestris, the style which never leaves the ground, that he chooses for his model. Pope's peculiar excellence as a letter-writer, in which difficult art he has been surpassed only by Gray, who had more learning, and Byron, who had more wit, is closely connected with his mundane wisdom, his inveterate habit of delivering himself like a man of this world. No wonder that the England of Pope was Voltaire's ideal, without superstition, without enthusiasm, without spirituality, with complete freedom for every writer who did not attack the Government of the day. The one really religious man in the circle of Pope and Swift was Addison, whose piety is essentially rational. He loved to show how reasonable Christianity was, how moderate, how gentle, how well bred. So with Pope's Deism, which hardly complied with the standards of the Roman Catholic Church. It was because his creed naturally commended itself to the minds of educated people, that Pope offered that creed for their acceptance. Swift applied the test of ridicule to the religion of others, and said as little as possible about his own. Berkeley was an exception. He had an imaginative, as well as a philosophical, intellect. He is our English Plato. But upon the men of Queen Anne he made no impression, and his philosophy conveyed no more to the mind of Swift than the music of Handel conveyed to his senses. He, the most powerful writer of the age, could no more distinguish Berkeley from Malebranche, than he could distinguish Handel from Buononcini. Swift in his prime was common sense personified. Except when in the blind rage of the party hack he imputed cowardice to Marlborough, his humour saved him from absurdity. He and his pupil Arbuthnot, who could write almost exactly like him, were never tired of making fun out of bombast, as Prior did out of Boileau's foolish ode on the capture of Namur. Arbuthnot was essentially a good-natured man, and a Tory by conviction, whereas no one could attribute either conviction or good nature to Swift. It is the more remarkable that they should have agreed in their pitiless satire of everything extravagant or high-flown. Pope compressed Newton into a neat couplet, and tossed off Bacon in a single line. He has expended far more eloquence upon his patron Robert Harley, Earl of Oxford, and even upon the Earl of Rochester's grandson, Lord Cornbury. The adroitest and most graceful of flatterers, the most poisonous and malignant of traducers. Pope was never led by any generous emotion to depart from the golden mediocrity, the rule of "not to admire," which suited his age and himself. The great and lasting service which he and Swift, and Addison and Steele, performed for literature, was to redeem it from slovenliness, to give it a form as correct as Racine's or Voltaire's. Dry den, though himself usual Iv restrained by his own sanity and judgment, had encouraged by his exuberance the vagaries of others, and Swift's youthful efforts to emulate Pindar are but a caricature of the general looseness that was setting in. Swift himself became afterwards a model of correct versification. But it was Pope who established once for all the reign of law in metre and rhyme. If some of his successors chose to fancy that nothing more was needed in poetry than accurate metre and regular rhyme, that was not the fault of Pope.

Pope, it must be remembered, was under the pervading influence of Horace. With Homer, who is all nature and sublimity, he had nothing in common. He sympathized instinctively with Horatian methods, at least in the Horatian Satires and Epistles. The Odes he left to Prior, who also was steeped in Horace, and had to persuade Cloe that she need not be jealous of Lydia. Est modus in rebus, sunt certi denique fines, might be taken as the motto of Queen Anne literature, except where love-making is concerned. Pope and his school worshipped moderation, looking upon enthusiasm with a supercilious sneer. In spite of Prior's irreverence, they set great store by Boileau, and paid almost as much respect to French models as Horace paid to Greek. Yet they wrote the vernacular. Pope is a well of English undefiled. At a time when Shakespeare was either neglected, or mauled by the gross taste of Colley Cibber, and Milton was abhorred, except by Addison, as a Republican Dissenter, Pope's epigrams and phrases passed into common speech and language. The Spectator, for which every one who professed any literary taste subscribed, had taught even before Pope, through Steele and Addison, that nothing could be good in any way which was not in good taste. Profanity was in bad taste. So was ostentation. So was vice. The furious diatribe of Collier was not half so effective in promoting virtue, which certainly needed promotion in 1711 and 1712, as Addison's quiet scorn of everything base, vulgar, and profane. He never reached, nor attempted to reach, the lower orders. He scarcely realized their existence, and probably thought that the clergy must deal with them.

His aim was to make goodness and piety modish, to turn the laugh against the other side. He was the best of good company, Lady Mary Wortley thought the best in the world. Lord Carteret contrasted him in that respect with Steele. They were both, he said, the most agreeable of companions at dinner. But Steele shone more brightly at the beginning, and Addison at the end. For by the time that Steele had drunk himself down, Addison had drunk himself up. Addison's convivial intemperance, the only kind of which he could be accused, was the vice of a shy man, whose tongue wine unlocked. To none of his contemporaries would it have been imputed as a fault at all. It is only because Addison resembled "a parson in a tie-wig," that any account was taken of the number of bottles he consumed. They cannot have affected him much in the morning. His head must have been very clear and cool when he described Sir Roger and Will Honeycomb.

Jonathan Swift is an apparent exception to the rule of mediocrity which marks the reign of Anne. Swift's genius was in some respects peculiar. His misanthropy was of later growth, or at least of later development. His sardonic humour was congenital; and the fierce indignation of which he boasted on his tombstone was excited by what appeared to him the hypocrisy of mankind. To Swift it was hypocrisy if a weak woman showed a little more sorrow for the death of a friend than she really felt. As a writer of prose or verse he fell in with the temper of his time by the closeness of his reasoning, and the sobriety of his style. Any kind of religious excitement moved his bitter scorn. Of hero-worship he was incapable, and he could not understand why the man who won the battle of Blenheim should be spared by the scribes of the party to which he was opposed. That Swift as an Englishman owed his liberty and independence to Marlborough, did not occur to him, or did not strike him as relevant. It would have been sham, cant, heroics, to take account of such sentimentality. The supreme art of Swift was in strict accordance with the rational, sceptical, positive spirit of the age. He had the gift, perhaps in fuller measure than any other controversialist, ancient or modern, of putting one side of a case so simply, forcibly, and clearly that there seemed to be no other. The Conduct of the Allies is one striking instance of this peculiar talent. The Letter to the October Club is another. Both pamphlets were written to order. On neither subject is it likely that Swift had any strong opinion of his own. In both cases, however, the argument is put from his employers' point of view with such masterly clearness, precision, and emphasis that it does not even seem to be one-sided. In the Conduct of the Allies, he had to prove that Holland and the Empire profited by a war for which England paid. In his Letter to the October Club, his theme was the impossibility of Harley and St. John having done more than they actually did to gratify the wishes of their followers. It would be difficult to imagine two more utterly different topics within the political sphere. Swift treats them both with the same ease, and with the same indefinable air of expert insight into every move of the game. Burke's magnificent treatise on the causes of discontent is far beyond the range of Swift in eloquence, in imagination, and in statesmanship. But Burke always rouses antagonism, never fails to suggest that there must be considerations which he ignores. What made Swift so consummately dexterous a controversialist was the dry light of cold reason which he shed upon the dispute. The slave of party as he was, no Professor of Mathematics could in appearance be more completely abstracted from all passion or prejudice than he. If anybody wants to see what Swift could be like when his self-love was wounded, and he really cared, let him read those awful verses on the Irish Parliament called The Legion Club. In Queen Anne's days, before his final retirement to Dublin, he wrote up Harley, and wrote down Marlborough, with as much semblance of impartiality as if he were proving a proposition of Euclid, with all the bias of an advocate, and all the dignity of a judge. The dignity was not genuine. Swift boasted of the rudeness which his cloth protected. He never knew his own place, and he was always trying to take somebody else's. It was only when he handled his pen, and became the man of letters, that his false pride fell away, and his intellect worked with unerring singleness of aim. He believed in neither Whigs nor Tories. He did not even believe in their honesty. The Tories had taken him up when the Whigs dropped him, and in serving the Tories he wreaked his vengeance on the Whigs. He exhausted his powers of sarcasm on the Irish bishops. The grapes were sour. He wanted to be a bishop himself. Yet, if Swift did not feel the restraint of his profession, he felt the influence of his time. He is never bombastic, never turgid, never obscure. His humour is never forced, always spontaneous, irrepressible, unexpected. His art is higher than Pope's because it conceals itself. Whether or no he actually said that "a man should write his own English," he acted upon the saying. Rabelais and La Rochefoucald were this strange parson's favourite reading. To them, to Cervantes, and to the classics of Greece and Rome, rather than to any English author, he was indebted for whatever was not original in his style. There is scarcely in all Swift's voluminous writings a single reference to Shakespeare, who was too great for the eighteenth century, and simply bewildered its critics. According to Spence, Pope enumerated the best English comedians as Etherege, Vanbrugh, Wycherley, Congreve, Fletcher, Jonson, and Shakespeare. Thomas Parnell, author of The Hermit, an Irish clergyman, who helped Pope in translating Homer, and drank himself to death after the loss of his wife, a martyr, as Spence quaintly says, to conjugal fidelity, was more in the correct line of poetry than the author of plays which Gibber then edited, and sonnets which nobody then read. Voltaire's opinion that Shakespeare is a barbarian was really the opinion of Pope, and Pope was the arbiter of taste. There is more wit in Love's Labour Lost than in all Pope, and yet if Love's Labour Lost were lost itself, the fame of Shakespeare would not appreciably suffer. The patient industry, the ingenious felicity, and the sound taste of Lewis Theobald, have done more than the editions of Pope, of Malone, or even of Johnson, to redeem the eighteenth century from the charge of ignoring what it could not understand.

Men of letters in Queen Anne's time were so closely connected with public life that their careers are part of history, and necessary to explain it. Swift was a far more practical statesman than Bolingbroke, and Harley lives not in the legislation of the period, but in the verse of Pope. Literature lasts when politics are forgotten, and hundreds know Prior as a poet, who would not recognize the Treaty of Utrecht under the name of "Matt's peace." And yet a biography of Prior, who was neither a professional politician nor a member of the governing class, would involve reference to the principal events both in William's reign and in Anne's. His patron was the magnificent Dorset, Charles Sackville, author of that lovely song "To all you ladies now on land," and the patron also of Dryden. Educated at Westminster and Cambridge, a Fellow of St. John's the great Tory-college, Prior went early into the diplomatic service, and acted as secretary at the Hague in the negotiations which concluded William's campaigns with the Treaty of Ryswick. Four years later he became member for East Grinstead in the last Parliament summoned by William of Orange, and on the accession of Anne he joined the Tory party. His political convictions were skin-deep, but he knew on which side his bread was buttered, and Toryism under Anne was in the long run the creed that paid. "Prior," said Pope in his candid-friendly way, "was less fit for business than even Addison, though he piqued himself much upon his talents for it." That was not the opinion of Prior's employers. Whig or Tory, Halifax or Bolingbroke. It was not the opinion of Swift. Nor would Prior have been sent, as he was, on delicate and difficult errands if he had merited Pope's malignant sneer. At the outset of his career Prior made the mistake of premature anticipation. The triumph of the Tories was not yet, and the Whigs took from him his Commissionership of Trade. Not till 1711, when Oxford had succeeded Godolphin, was he again taken into public employment, and made a Commissioner of Customs. The Whigs treated him more hardly than the Tories treated Congreve, for whose Commissionership of Licenses Halifax interceded with Harley in 1708, and received the Virgilian answer

"Non obtusa adeo gesiamus pectora Poeni,
Nee tarn aversus equos Tyria sol jungit ab urbe."

In 1711 Prior suddenly found himself at the very centre of affairs, plunged into business of the highest national and European importance. While Marlborough was in the Netherlands, preparing to renew the campaign and outmanoeuvre Villars, Louis made overtures of peace to Great Britain through de Torcy and Gaultier. These proposals were communicated to Heinsius at the Hague by Lord Raby, created Earl of Strafford with the title of his great-uncle Wentworth. Heinsius, not unnaturally annoyed, attempted to deal on his own account with the French King. This unsuccessful effort was made in April, and in July Lord Oxford, never precipitate, thought that the time had come for a special mission to France. The utmost secrecy was observed, not merely in fraud of the public, but with the more particular object of deceiving the Duke of Marlborough. Oxford and St. John looked about them for a trusty and skilful envoy who could accompany Gaultier. Their choice fell upon Matthew Prior. It must be borne in mind that Prior was a professional diplomatist, not merely a man of letters. But his friendship with St. John arose from common tastes, and to patronize genius without condescension was Oxford's worthiest aim. Prior amply justified the confidence reposed in him. His enterprise was full of difficulty, and not unattended with danger. At first his course was smooth. He crossed with Gaultier from Dover to Calais in a fishing-boat, and was well received at Fontainebleau. De Torcy had known him at the Embassy in Paris, and Prior was just the sort of Englishman that Frenchmen liked. The British demands, however, were not such as de Torcy could have pleasure in submitting to his royal master. So far as Spain and Philip of Anjou were concerned, St. John, or Prior, was not exacting. He would be satisfied with a stipulation, as easy to grant as it would be easy to break, that the same person should never inherit the French and Spanish Crowns. A much more practical, and a much less flexible, demand was that Spain should give Great Britain in all commercial matters the terms of the most favoured nation. For, while Louis had at one time supposed France to be invincible in war, he had never cherished the delusion, at least since he revoked the Edict of Nantes, that his subjects could compete on equal terms with Englishmen in affairs of trade. Another formidable demand Prior had also been instructed (perhaps at his own suggestion) to put forward at the same time. The right of supplying the Spanish plantations with negro slaves must be transferred from the French company, which then held it, to the hands of British merchants. Besides these economic advantages, real or imaginary, some territorial concessions were prescribed. Spain was to yield Gibraltar and Port Mahon. Newfoundland and Hudson's Bay were to be surrendered by France. Prior supported these proposals with a vigour and ability which entirely refute the malice of Pope. England, he said, had not the least desire to injure the prosperity of other nations. Monopolies were bad for every one. Free trade was good for all. The Spaniards had misemployed their exclusive powers, and it was time that these should be shared by more enlightened communities. If the Archduke Charles were King of Spain, he would readily grant the commercial facilities required. If the right of Philip were acknowledged, the least he could do in return would be to prove himself as liberal as Charles. Mr. Frederick Wyon, in his valuable History of Great Britain during the Reign of Queen Anne, sarcastically observes that Charles might well promise what he could not perform, and that the Allies, having failed to drive Philip from Spain, could scarcely expect to be put in the same position as if they had succeeded. This is a fallacy. There was one war, not two wars, and the Spaniards were in the same boat with the French. Even in Spain Gibraltar had been taken by Rooke. But the victories of Blenheim, Ramillles, Oudenarde, and Malplaquet were quite as material to the issue as if they had been won upon Spanish soil. Marlborough, not Peterborough, had made this country the master of the situation.

Prior was not a Plenipotentiary. If the terms offered through him were rejected, he could only go home, and report the failure of his mission. Louis, however, was unwilling to break off negotiations. Believing that he could induce the British Government to moderate their demands, he appointed a representative of his own to accompany Prior. Accustomed during a long life to lean upon the exertions of others, and to appropriate the fruits of their successes, Louis had acquired an insight into character which would have been more remarkable in a private man. On this occasion he selected a merchant of Rouen, Menager by name, who not only understood the West Indian trade, but was also an adroit and prudent diplomatist. And now Prior approached the most perilous part of his adventures. Hitherto inviolable secrecy had been preserved. But England was not France. For fifteen years there had been no censorship of the Press, and the editor of the Daily Courant was on the look-out for news. Ever since the dismissal of Godolphin the Whigs had been seeking without finding an opportunity for revenge. They could not hope for a better chance than the discovery of the business which brought Menager to London with Prior. Accident favoured them. Early in August, Prior, Menager, and Gaultier landed at Deal. Their too obvious anxiety to elude notice excited the suspicion of the local magistrates, who had them followed, and arrested them at Canterbury. They were, of course, released by an order from the Secretary of State, so soon as St. John heard of their mishap. But it was too late. Prior, though he gave another name, had been recognized by an officer of the customs at Deal, and the story was at once published not merely in London, but also in Amsterdam. The public, however, had not discovered much. Nothing was known of Menager, and even Swift, who prided himself on the especial accuracy of his information, was completely in the dark. Menager was privately presented to the Queen, who received him graciously, but he was directed to remain in his lodgings during the day, and to take the air at night. He held nocturnal meetings, most of them at Prior's house, with Oxford, St. John, Shrewsbury, Dartmouth, and Jersey. Edward Villiers, first Earl of Jersey, who then held the office of Lord Chamberlain, was a Jacobite, and in the pay of France. He died, however, on the 26th of August, and his colleagues were in no hurry to alter the proposals already made. Menager tried in vain to elicit from the English statesmen how far they would support the demands of the Empire and of the Dutch States. Oxford and St. John were not the kind of men to risk their own necks, or to trust the mercy of their political opponents. While they were havering about the fortifications of Dunkirk, the secrecy of their interview was maintained, and even when Menager took leave of the Queen at the end of September, he was brought to her room in Windsor Castle by the back stairs. It was not till the 13th of October that the Daily Courant obtained from the Minister of the Empire, Count Gallas, to whom they had been confidentially imparted, the preliminary articles of peace.

They appeared at an unlucky moment, four days after the arrival at Spithead of the squadron despatched under Admiral Sir Hovenden Walker and General Hill to take Quebec. General Hill was Mrs. Masham's brother, a totally incompetent person, whom Marlborough had refused to promote. His expedition had ignominiously failed, the French were confirmed in their hold upon Canada, and now it transpired that the Government were prepared to throw away the fruits of the war by recognizing the grandson of Louis as King of Spain. To get rid of Count Gallas by handing him his passports was simple enough. He had abused his position by a breach of confidence, and had acted as an open ally of one political party in the State to which he was accredited. But no enforcement of diplomatic regularity, however justifiable, could make it popular to surrender what Marlborough had won while Marlborough himself was actually in the field.

Prior had served the Government faithfully, and was not responsible for carrying out his instructions. When the Peace Congress was appointed to meet at Utrecht on the 1st of January, 1712, Lord Oxford desired that Prior should be named a third Plenipotentiary with Bishop Robinson of Bristol, Lord Privy Seal, and the Earl of Strafford. Strafford, however, was what we now call a snob, and objected to being associated with a man of Prior's plebeian origin. A modern Minister would have dispensed with the services of the nobleman who had troubled him on such frivolous grounds. Oxford, perhaps under pressure from the Queen, withdrew the name of the only Plenipotentiary who is remembered, or worth remembering, now. St. John at least had no sympathy with the vulgarity of the foolish Earl. When at the close of the Session of 1712 he had been created Viscount Bolingbroke, as a reward for services which it would have been difficult to specify, he started for Paris to settle with de Torcy the questions not solved at Utrecht. His companions were Prior, and the inevitable Gaultier, a Catholic and a thoroughgoing Jacobite. Bolingbroke, who loved mystery, resorted to pseudonyms. But by this time Prior's face was familiar both at Dover and at Calais. Even if he had really wished to escape recognition, which may be doubted, Bolingbroke would certainly have failed. He was received with acclamations, which were intended quite as much for Prior as for him. This time it was arranged without any difficulty that Philip should renounce the throne of France, that the French Bourbons should renounce the throne of Spain, and that in default of heirs to Philip the Spanish Crown should devolve upon the Duke of Savoy, who would have Sicily for his pains, with the title of King. That the inhabitants of Sicily, or

Spain, or France had anything to do with these prospective arrangements would have been regarded as preposterous both by Bolingbroke and by Prior. A very different objection occurred to them. How would these renunciations be enforced? Louis himself had broken most of the engagements he made. Why should his kinsfolk and descendants be more scrupulous than himself? Bolingbroke suggested that the States General should be convoked, and should ratify the pledges of the Royal family. Louis would, of course, listen to no such proposal. A great many things had to happen before a King of France admitted that there was any French institution not subordinate to himself. Louis had been much elated by the successes of Villars in the absence of Marlborough. He received Bolingbroke with the most flattering attention, feeling instinctively that if this man had been at the head of affairs in England, France would still be the first military power in Europe, and the Treaty of Utrecht would have been another Treaty of Dover. The States General were not to be mentioned. Englishmen did not understand France. But Louis could rely upon Bolingbroke to help him against Marlborough, and the English charlatan, who was worth far more to France than the costly diamond given him by Louis, went home to proclaim a truce of four months, which was celebrated by several bonfires. Prior, who had received the King's portrait set in diamonds, remained in charge of the Embassy at Paris. The correspondence between him and Bolingbroke when not strictly official was affectionate and familiar. It was "my dear Harry" and "my dear Matt." Madame de Parabère, who must have been strangely uncomfortable at the Court of Madame de Maintenon, was taught in the more congenial company of Prior to drink the healths of "Harre et Robin," Henry Lord Bolingbroke and Robert Lord Oxford. Shrewsbury was despatched to sign the treaty. Prior stayed at Paris so long as Queen Anne lived. At her death he was recalled in disgrace, being too much implicated in Bolingbroke's designs for bringing over the Pretender to be employed by a Whig Minister or a Hanoverian Sovereign. But while his own party were in power, he was trusted by Bolingbroke, and perhaps by Oxford, with secrets which might have brought them to the block. Jonathan Swift was a man of very different calibre from Prior's. Although he sometimes descended to write for his party what he must have known was nonsense, he had the mind of a statesman, and would have been a far better Minister than either St. John or Harley. Swift lived in politics, and was a clergyman merely by accident. He was only twenty-six when Sir William Temple sent him to urge upon the King his arguments in favour of the Triennial Bill. Swift's dependent position in the household of Temple had inspired him with a ferocious hatred of all persons in authority who did not show him personal respect. He came to London in 1705 at the age of thirty-eight, already a disappointed man. Temple had died without doing anything for him, and Temple was a Whig. What would the other Whigs do? They did not care for parsons, and they did nothing. Swift had been at school with Congreve, then at the height of his literary fame. Congreve made him acquainted with Charles Montague Halifax, the Whig Maecenas of the age. But Halifax was out of office, and his successor Godolphin knew more about race horses than literature. Swift went back to his benefice in Ireland a sad and sour man. But it was not until he returned to London in 1707 on the business of Queen Anne's Bounty, which he wished to extend to Ireland, that he discovered the full iniquity of which Whigs were capable. They took little interest in Queen Anne's Bounty, or in the Irish Church, or in the Reverend Jonathan Swift. He left England in deep disgust, and attacked the Irish Presbyterians in his Letter on the Sacramental Test. Next time he came to London, in 1710, when the Journal to Stella begins, he was more successful. The Tories, especially St. John, took him up, settled his business, and secured him as their scribe for the remainder of Anne's reign. It may be doubted whether any Englishman has ever wielded more practical and immediate influence with his pen than Swift exercised during this period. He could appeal to any class of readers, from the highest to the lowest. He never missed his point, or failed in controversy to get home. He never shrank from attacking greatness, as in Marlborough, or valour, as in Cutts, or virtue, as in Somers. He feared no man's intellect, and he was too much engrossed in his subject to think of the ultimate consequences to which his proposals might lead. The Journal to Stella begins with his arrival at Chester on his way from Dublin in September 1710. Godolphin had just been removed from office, and Parliament was about to be dissolved. When the General Election had confirmed Harley and St. John in power, they turned to Swift as their best penman, and he fought their battles in the Examiner. Swift was an ideal journalist. He was always clear, forcible, and persuasive; never hazy, ambiguous, or obscure. He wrote the best English, scholar's English, free from foreign idioms, cant phrases, mannerisms, and tricks of style. His humour preserved him from the temptation to fine writing, and enabled him to put the case of his opponents in a ludicrous shape. His audacity has never been surpassed. In November

1710 he gravely argued that the best means of paying for the war would be the repudiation of the national debt. Swift was strictly honest in private life, and punctilious in the discharge of pecuniary obligations. Yet he could make a flagrantly dishonest proposal in a public journal, because it would be popular with the party he served. The national debt, like the standing army, was Whig. Country gentlemen had no money in the funds, and the landed interest regarded commercialism as the enemy. Therefore the clerical moralist, who knew perfectly well the meaning of what he said, calmly suggested a clean slate as the policy, not of a Turkish, but of a British, Administration. Harley, a Downing Street man if ever there was one, cannot have regarded as serious Swift's proposal for the repeal of the eighth commandment. His own way of raising funds was a lottery, which the public opinion of the time did not condemn. He was, no doubt, willing enough that his predecessors should be attacked as rogues and traitors for upholding the honour of their country, and paying her debts by fair means. Swift did not stop there. He counted the price of Marlborough's glories, elaborately comparing his salaries, pensions, and Parliamentary grants with the laurel crown and the copper medals of a Roman conqueror. No man was a hero to Swift, and no hero has been more open to criticism than Marlborough. But by this satire, clever as it is, the writer did himself more harm than he did the Duke, and the ribald parson who wrote the Tale of a Tub seemed a strange champion for defenders of the Church.

Swift's social success, however, was quite as great as his political services were valuable. Although he seldom smiled, and never laughed, his drollery was irresistible, and his eccentric behaviour added to the joke. Harley and St. John flattered him by calling him Jonathan. He lived, dined, and in his sober way drank, with the wits. Prior became his constant companion. Addison, who seldom let politics interfere with friendship, delighted in Swift's sardonic humour, so unlike his own. Pope looked up to him with an awe and reverence which he felt for no other human being. Arbuthnot trumpeted his fame, and copied his style. They even endured his puns, in which Swift, unlike most genuine humourists, took great pleasure. Many of these were execrable, as he frankly admitted himself, protesting that he learned the trick from Stella. The best that survives is a Latin one. A lady had knocked a violin off a table with the sleeve of her mantle. Swift quoted, with exquisite neatness —

"Mantua vae miserae nimium vicina Cremonae."

Swift had a curious fascination for women. He puzzled, amused, and frightened them. He differed from other men, for he never made love. He had no home life. If the fine ladies of his acquaintance heard of the mysterious friend in Ireland, they would have been attracted all the more. Swift showed them no mercy. It was not in his nature to be chivalrous. He felt no respect for women, unless they had minds, and used them. But he would talk in a boudoir by the hour, and write comic verses by the hundred for the mistress of it, if the fancy took him. His Verses, Wrote on a Lady's Ivory Table-Book are worth quoting, not merely for their excellence, but also because they show what Swift really thought of the other sex.

"Peruse my leaves through every part,
And think thou sees my Owner's Heart,
Scrawled o'er with Trifles thus, and quite
As hard, as senseless, and as light;
Exposed to every coxcomb's eyes,
But hid with caution from the wise.
Here you may read (Dear charming Saint),
Beneath (A new Receipt for Paint):
Here in Beau-spelling (tru tel deth).
There in her own (for an el breth).
Here (Lovely Nymph pronounce my Doom),
There (a safe Way to use Perfume);
Here a page filled with Billet-Doux;
On t'other side (laid out for shoes):
(Madam, I die without your grace),
Item, (for half a yard of lace)
Who that had wit would place it here,
For every peeping Fop to jeer?

Whoe'er expects to hold his part
In such a Book, and such a Heart,
If he be wealthy, and a Fool,
Is in all points the fittest Tool;
Of whom it may be justly said.
He's a Gold Pencil tipped with Lead.

Of Swift's ways with men there are endless stories. Perhaps the best and most characteristic is Pope's experience as recorded by Spence:

"One evening Gay and I went to see him: you know how intimately we were all acquainted. On our coming in: 'Heyday, gentlemen,' says the doctor, 'what's the meaning of this visit? How come you to leave all the great lords, that you are so fond of, to come hither to see a poor dean?' 'Because we would rather see you than any of them.' 'Ay, any one that did not know you so well as I do might believe you. But, since you are come, I must get some supper for you, I suppose?' 'No, doctor, we have supped already.' 'Supped already! that's impossible; why, 'tis not eight o'clock yet.' 'Indeed we have.' 'That's very strange: but if you had not supped, I must have got something for you. Let me see, what should I have had? a couple of lobsters? ay, that would have done very well; — two shillings; tarts: a shilling. But you will drink a glass of wine with me, though you supped so much before your usual time, only to spare my pocket?' 'No, we had rather talk with you than drink with you.' 'But if you had supped with me, as in all reason you ought to have done, you must have drunk with me. A bottle of wine: two shillings. Two and two is four; and one is five; just two and sixpence a piece. There, Pope, there's half a crown for you; and there's another for you, sir: for I won't save anything by you, I am determined.' This was all said and done with his usual seriousness on such occasions; and in spite of everything we could say to the contrary, he actually obliged us to take the money."

It is impossible always to believe Pope, he told so many lies, usually from pure love of mystification. But this story is too odd not to be true. No one, not even Pope, would have thought of inventing it. We may perhaps feel doubtful whether Pope quite understood Swift's meaning. Swift, of course, knew his own reputation for narrowness, and suspected his visitors of conspiring to save him the expense of their entertainment. His pride was touched, and he would not take advantage of their early meal. Yet still the ruling passion was strong. The quantity of wine suggested was remarkably small for the age of Anne. Swift's oddities must have been heightened by the gown and bands which he habitually wore. He was below the middle height, his garb was not at that time held in high esteem, but Swift himself was universally dreaded for his temper and his tongue. Although he disliked and despised most of his brother clergymen, he insisted that the clerical profession should be treated in his presence with respect. When he closed his series of articles for the Examiner with the prorogation of Parliament in 1711, he might boast that he had turned the tables against the Whigs. He had made many people believe that Marlborough fought for his own hand, that Godolphin plundered the nation, and that Harley was a stern, unbending patriot, a "soul supreme." One instance will prove the lengths to which Swift would go in exalting Tories over Whigs. It is the almost inconceivably loathsome copy of verses called Description of a Salamander, and published in 1711 . Salamander Cutts, John Lord Cutts of Gowran in the Irish Peerage, distinguished himself at the battle of Blenheim, and was famous for his coolness under fire, whence his nickname. But he was also a Whig Member of Parliament, and therefore Swift, four years after his death, assailed him with a venomous scurrility which he would certainly not have used while Cutts was alive. When the dead man's sister complained to the Lord Treasurer, Swift loftily advised his patron to take no heed of such trifles. He was not even ashamed of mentioning the Salamander to Stella. Swift's greatest service to the Tory party, greater even than his Letter to the October Club, was his Conduct of the Allies. So far as it protested against a continuance of the war, it was unanswerable, and served the interests of the nation no less than the prospects of the Tories. His satirical ballad on Daniel Finch, Earl of Nottingham, which begins with the words "An Orator dismal of Nottinghamshire, who had forty years let out his conscience for hire," though it enraged Nottingham himself, made both Whigs and Tories laugh at the pomposity of that tiresome pedant, who was, however, a perfectly honest man, as Swift must have known. The Duchess of Somerset, from her singular hold upon the Queen, was a more formidable enemy. Swift called her an insinuating woman, and was never tired of demanding that the Lord Treasurer should remove her from the Court. Oxford, however, was pretty well convinced that if he made any such attempt he was far more likely to be removed than she. The Duke, who was always intriguing, he did succeed in dismissing from the Cabinet before the end of 1711. The Duchess, so long as Anne lived, was immoveable. If Abigail Masham's rank had been higher, she might have succeeded the Duchess of Marlborough as Mistress of the Robes. But Anne was a stickler for precedent and custom. Her Mistress of the Robes must be a Duchess, and even a Percy was not too proud to take the post. Once there, the Duchess of Somerset knew how to make herself indispensable, often as Swift might vent his spleen upon "Carrots from Northumberland." When he thought of "Carrots," even in writing to Stella, he cursed and swore. His entry for the 9th of December, 1711, gives a vivid picture of the terror which her Grace inspired in him, and the many victims of his pen would have been consoled if they could have seen how their persecutor shivered, the man who accused Marlborough of cowardice.

"I was this morning with the Secretary (St. John); we are both of opinion that the Queen is false. I told him what I heard, and he confirmed it by other circumstances. I then went to my friend Lewis (Erasmus Lewis, the diplomatist), who had sent to see me. He talks of nothing but retiring to his estate in Wales. He gave me reasons to believe the whole matter is settled between the Queen and the Whigs; he hears that Lord Somers is to be Treasurer, and believes that, sooner than turn out the Duchess of Somerset, she will dissolve the Parliament, and get a Whiggish one, which may be done by managing elections. Things are now in the crisis, and a day or two will determine. I have desired him to engage Lord Treasurer, that as soon as he finds the change is resolved on, he will send me abroad as Queen's Secretary somewhere or other, where I may remain till the new Ministers recall me; and then I will be sick for five or six months, till the storm has spent itself. I hope he will grant me this; for I should hardly trust myself to the mercy of my enemies while their anger is fresh. I dined to-day with the Secretary, who affects mirth, and seems to hope all will yet be well. I took him aside after dinner, told him how I had served them and had asked no reward, but thought I might ask security; and then desired the same thing of him, to send me abroad before a change. He embraced me, and swore he would take the same care of me as himself, etc., but bid me have courage, for that in two days my Lord Treasurer's wisdom would appear greater than ever; that he suffered all that had happened on purpose, and had taken measures to turn it to advantage. I said 'God send it;' but do not believe a syllable; and, as far as I can judge, the game is lost. I shall know more soon and my letters will at least be a good history to show you the steps of this change."

St. John never took quite such good care of any one else as he took of himself. But he was habitually kind to Swift, and on this occasion Oxford joined in reassuring that faint heart. Swift's idea of a diplomatic appointment, which may have been suggested by the despatch of Bishop Robinson to Utrecht, came to nothing, and was not seriously regarded by his friends. His immediate fears were quieted on the 29th of December, 1711, when the Queen agreed to the creation of twelve new Peers, and the Duchess of Somerset was forgotten. The charge of double dealing, often made by Swift against Anne, who hated him, during these transactions, seems to be unfounded. The Queen stood by her Tory Ministers to the point of turning out the Duke of Marlborough, and even the Duke of Somerset. The Duchess of Somerset she retained on private and personal grounds, such as Queen Victoria pleaded when she refused to part with her Ladies of the Bedchamber in 1839. Somerset himself had the honour of following, though not of accompanying, Marlborough. It is amusing to find that Swift wrote, when Marlborough was dismissed, "I do not love to see personal resentment mix with public affairs." Swift's vivid insight into other people's characters did not extend to his own.

His reward was not the diplomatic one he expected. His Journal to Stella closes with his departure for Ireland in May 1713, to be installed in the Deanery of St. Patrick's, which had been conferred upon him in April. He then considered his friends to be safe in office, and regarded himself, not without reason, as the cause of their being still there. The time had come to think of his own prospects. Swift's ambition had no sordid taint. His habits were simple and frugal. He was generous to Stella and Mrs. Dingley. He was quite content to be poor. But he was conscious of immeasurable superiority to all the bishops and other clergymen of his acquaintance. He expected and demanded ecclesiastical promotion from the Government which he had served as faithfully and unscrupulously as Cardinal Wolsey served Henry the Eighth. If the Government had been able to do exactly as they pleased, Swift would probably have been first Bishop of Hereford, and then Archbishop of York. The Archbishop of York, John Sharp, who died in 1714, was a favourite with Queen Anne, and did not conceal his opinion that Swift was quite unfit to be a bishop. Swift always believed that Sharp prevented his appointment to Hereford, but it is doubtful whether the Queen would have allowed it in any case. Her Majesty looked upon Swift as an obscene atheist who disgraced his gown, and to argue with her was like arguing with a mantelpiece or a stone wall. Happily for Swift an Irish see became vacant at the beginning of 1713. The Queen would indeed by no means consent that he should have it, or a Canonry of Windsor, which also fell in at the same time. But the Dean of St. Patrick's was ready to become Bishop of Dromore, and the patronage of the Deanery belonged by custom to the Duke of Ormond as Lord Lieutenant. So the bargain was struck without prejudice to the virtue of good Queen Anne. One last service Dean Swift rendered to his patrons, and his gratitude on this occasion was certainly no sense of favours to come. His Public Spirit of the Whigs, published in 1714, was an answer to Steele's Crisis, for which a Tory House of Commons expelled the author. Swift might have suffered a more severe punishment than expulsion if he had not concealed his authorship of this pamphlet with unusual care. For it consisted chiefly of an attack upon the Union with Scotland, written in language studiously insulting to the Scottish nation. "Imagine," he said, "a person of quality prevailed upon to marry a woman much his inferior and without a groat to her fortune, and her friends arguing that she was as good as her husband because she brought him as numerous a family of poor relations and servants as she found in his house." The reckless malignity of this and similar gibes was denounced by the House of Lords as a scandalous and seditious libel. The Queen offered a reward of three hundred pounds for the name of the author, which was never publicly divulged, and Oxford, after falsely telling the Lords that he did not know who wrote the pamphlet, sent Swift a bank bill for a hundred pounds.

The Public Spirit of the Whigs is discreditable to Swift's patriotism. He knew better than to suppose that England was injured by the Union with Scotland. On one point, however, it does help to clear his fame. He has been accused of being a party to Jacobite intrigues while he professed, like Atterbury, allegiance to Queen Anne. No Jacobite would, in 1714, have gone out of his way to express scorn and contempt for the only part of Great Britain from which the Pretender could look for any support. That Swift was incapable of subterfuge under stress of personal danger cannot be affirmed by any one acquainted with the whole of his career. But he was habitually veracious, and his word was his bond. It is weak men, not strong men, who tell lies. Two years after everything was over, when Swift had retired finally to Dublin, and left the strife of British politics, so far as they did not concern Ireland, for ever, on the 22nd of November, 1716, Archbishop King of Dublin wrote to him from London on ecclesiastical business, and concluded his letter with these significant words: "We have a strong Report that my Lord Bolingbroke will return here, and be pardoned; certainly it must not be for Nothing. I hope he can tell no ill story of you." To this letter Swift at once replied. King was one of the few people he respected, and he is supposed to have trusted the archbishop with the secret of his life. The first part of this familiar epistle is taken up with protestations of Bolingbroke's innocence, which were quite sincere, because the writer did not know the truth, then only known at St. Germains. There follows this solemn and emphatic passage: "But, whether I am mistaken or no in other men, I beg your Grace to believe that I am not mistaken in myself. I always professed to be against the Pretender; and am so still. And this is not to make my Court (which I know is vain) for I own myself full of Doubts, Fears, and Dissatisfactions; which I think on as seldom as I can: yet, if I were of any Value, the Public may safely rely on my Loyalty; because I look upon the coming of the Pretender as a greater evil than we are like to suffer under the worst Whig Ministry that can be found." Swift ends this letter with the words "I beg your Grace's blessing." It seems to me beyond all question sincere; and, if so, it proves that Swift was never a Jacobite. Throughout his public career he always maintained that the Tories were not Jacobites, but true Church of England men, and that the Queen detested the Pretender, whom, though he was her father's son, she never knew. To suppose Swift a Jacobite is to suppose him as dishonest as Bolingbroke and as stupid as Oxford. He was not a scrupulous politician. But at treason and Popery he drew the line. Bolingbroke concealed from him the essential circumstance of his own intrigues with the Pretender, knowing his friend's regard for "the Security of the Protestant Succession in the House of Hanover: not from any partiality to that illustrious House, further than as it hath had the honour to mingle with the Blood Royal of England." In a melancholy retrospect, called Some Idle Thoughts upon the Present State of Affairs, and referring to the year 1714, Swift took leave of the busy scene where he had played so powerful and conspicuous a part. "It may serve," he wrote, "for a great lesson of Humiliation to mankind to behold the Habits and Passions of Men otherwise highly accomplished triumphing over Interest, Friendship, Honour, and their own personal Safety, as well as that of their Country; and probably of a most gracious Princess who hath entrusted it to them. A Ship's Crew quarrelling in a Storm, or while their Enemies are within Gunshot, is but a faint idea of this fatal infatuation." The reign of Anne could have no more fitting epilogue than this masterly little essay, which Swift wrote from his retirement in Berkshire after the failure of his efforts to reconcile Oxford and Bolingbroke. The real Swift cannot be better expressed than in the words which he wrote to his fondest admirer Pope on the 27t?h of September, 1725: "I have ever hated all nations, professions, and communities, and all my love is towards individuals: for instance, I hate the tribe of lawyers, but I love counsellor such a one, and judge such a one. It is so with physicians (I will not speak of my own trade), soldiers, English, Scotch, French, and the rest. But principally I hate and detest that animal called man; although I heartily love John, Peter, Thomas, and so forth. This is the system upon which I have governed myself many years (but do not tell) and so I shall go on till I have done with them. I have got materials toward a treatise proving the falsity of that definition animal rationale, and to show it should be only rationis capax. Upon this great foundation of misanthropy (though not in Timon's manner) the whole building of my travels is erected; and I never will have peace of mind, till all honest men are of my opinion: by consequence you are to embrace it immediately, and procure that all who deserve my esteem may do so too. The matter is so clear, that it will admit of no dispute; nay, I will hold a hundred pounds that you and I agree on the point." That is the true key to the meaning of Gulliver's Travels, and to the nature of Jonathan Swift.

A more striking contrast to the character of Swift could hardly be imagined than the character of Addison, whom every one that knew him loved, including Swift himself. Addison's influence upon politics, though far less than Swift's, is not to be despised. Always a staunch and consistent, though a rational and moderate, Whig, he received, soon after his election as a probationer fellow of Magdalen, a pension of three hundred a year from Halifax, then first Lord of the Treasury, that he might qualify himself for the diplomatic service by foreign travel. This was in 1699. When he returned from France and Italy, Germany and Holland, in 1703, Halifax had long been out of office, William the Third was dead, and Addison's pension had been stopped by the frugal Ministry of Godolphin. His very poor poem on Blenheim, however, was rewarded with a Commissionership; he was successively Under-Secretary of State to Sir Charles Hedges and to the Earl of Sunderland; and after the Whig victories at the polls in 1708, he became Chief Secretary to Wharton, Lord Lieutenant of Ireland. He was then Member for Malmesbury in the British House of Commons. At Westminster he never spoke, being unable to conquer his natural shyness, even when he became a Secretary of State under George the First. In the Irish House of Commons he did venture to address a smaller and quieter audience. But it is nevertheless true that no man of letters, before or since, has risen so high in politics as Addison by means of literary talent alone. It was while he lived in Ireland, with the uncongenial company of Wharton, that Addison began to write for Steele's Tatler, published on Tuesdays, Thursdays, and Saturdays, when the country post went out of London. Addison's articles in the Tatler are not as a rule political. It was after he and his friends had been turned out of office, in 1710, that he wrote for the Whig Examiner against Swift. Although the General Election crushed the Whigs, Addison was returned without opposition for Malmesbury, and Swift admitted, perhaps with excessive modesty, that in Addison as a political journalist he had for once found his match. During the months of 1711 and 1712, when the Spectator appeared, the Tories were in office and in power. The Spectator, though its two principal contributors were Addison and Steele, was not avowedly political. Sir Roger de Coverley, the Tory squire, took more hold upon the public than Sir Andrew Freeport, the Whig merchant. But Addison, whose exquisite tact prevented him from ever preaching out of season, lost no good opportunity of putting in a word for the Protestant Church and the House of Hanover. He was always true to his principles, and never deserted his colours. His tragedy of Cato, acted at Drury Lane in 1713, was treated by the Whigs as a Whig play, though the resemblance of Wharton, or even of Halifax, to Cato was far from obvious. Bolingbroke made a palpable hit by sending for Barton Booth, who played the title-part, and giving him fifty guineas, public money no doubt, for defending the cause of liberty against a perpetual dictatorship. The point was double-edged, because Caesar refused the proffered crown, whereas Marlborough had asked to be made Captain General for life. At the death of Anne, Addison was engaged upon the eighth volume of the Spectator, which he conducted during six months of its prosperous existence without the help of Steele. Steele himself, who became Member for Stockbridge, in Hampshire, at the General Election of 1713, did not shine as a politician. He was greeted on rising in the House of Commons with cries of "Tatler," which, though really compliments, were not so intended, and his expulsion from the House, scandalous as it was, would have been impossible if he had understood the temper of the assembly. This ignominious transaction is redeemed by a picturesque incident of a personal kind. The Earl of Nottingham's eldest son, Lord Finch, tried to speak for the first time on Steele's behalf. But nervousness sealed his lips, and as he sat down, he was heard to say, in artless language more cheered than any eloquence would have been, "It is strange that I cannot speak for this man, though I could readily fight for him." Steele had as many friends as faults, though he had a faculty for getting into scrapes which often tried his best friends hard. It is painful, on the other hand, to record, on the unimpeachable evidence of his own letters in the Portland Correspondence, that Daniel Defoe urged the Government to insist upon the expulsion of Steele. Defoe's character will not bear much scrutiny, or indeed any scrutiny at all. He was in Harley's pay, and he did what Harley told him to do, rather overacting the part than otherwise. His books, by which he lives, were none of them published in Queen Anne's reign. But his political influence was not the less strong or marked because it was exercised behind the scenes. In 1705 Harley sent him to Scotland, and his correspondence shows that he kept the Secretary of State exceedingly well informed about the temper of parties and the minds of men. Defoe was by inclination or conviction a Whig, and his zeal on behalf of Nonconformists had brought him to the pillory. The Presbyterianism of Scotland was not uncongenial to his taste. But in Edinburgh he was simply Harley's agent, giving him the information, so valuable to a Minister, about leading politicians and the way to win them. It was, for instance, from Defoe that Harley learnt how strong the feeling was in Edinburgh against English desertion of the Scottish colonists at Darien. Although Defoe was one of the greatest writers who ever used the English language, he did not belong to the literary circle of Swift and Addison and Pope. Pope said condescendingly, "that there was something good in all he had written." He was not more scrupulous, or more high-handed, than Pope himself. His political influence, which was all through Queen Anne's reign considerable, he wielded entirely and exclusively with his pen. His own principles were sound and enlightened, religious toleration and free trade being their corner-stones. If he was not always consistent, the explanation is that he varied with his patron Harley, who procured his release from prison in 1704, and always afterwards employed him as an agent or spy. For a long time he supported Marlborough and Godolphin in their policy of continuing the French war after Ramillies. He defended, from the Whig point of view, the impeachment of Sacheverell. But when Harley returned to office in 1710, he engaged Defoe to plead his cause in the Review, and that versatile disputant then went over to the cause of peace. Defoe never troubled himself about consistency, and he had no character to lose. The public devoured what he wrote without regard for his personality, because he had the gift of making the wildest fiction or the merest imagination look like sober truth, so that it was read by thousands and believed of course. His arguments, on the other hand, were convincing, and his grasp of economic science was unusual in his age. He had done much to allay the financial panic which followed the dismissal of Godolphin, by proving that the security for the public funds and the national debt was parliamentary, not ministerial, thus counteracting, so far as he could, the mischievous advocacy of repudiation to which Swift stooped. Defoe's Review was, as we have seen, killed by the statute against knowledge, the Stamp Act of 1712. But his pen could not be idle, and in 1713 his irony, surpassed only by Swift's, brought him again into misfortune, as it had led him to the pillory ten years before. Then, he had held the mirror up to High Churchmen by pretending to be one himself. Now, he wrote as a Jacobite, and the Jacobites did not like it at all. But it was the Whigs who, very foolishly, took action. Perhaps they had not forgiven Defoe for his able, though unsuccessful, support of that commercial treaty with France which was appended to the Treaty of Utrecht. They might certainly have known better than to suppose that his two pamphlets, called respectively Reasons against the Succession of the House of Hanover, and Considerations of the Advantages of the Pretender's possessing the Crown of Great Britain, meant what their titles implied. Defoe's object was purely satirical. He had no more wish to help the Pretender than Swift had to make the Irish people eat babies, or to abolish Christianity by law. But the Whigs were so much afraid of Jacobite plots that they felt like men living on a volcano, and Anne could not bear to be reminded of any successor, Jacobite or Hanoverian. Defoe was taught once more by practical experience how dangerous a gift the sense of humour may be. In this case its consequences could only be averted by a pardon under the Great Seal.

Defoe, however, did not stand alone among his contemporaries as a victim of transcendent gifts. The Deanery of St. Patrick's, that symbol of disappointed ambition, was far worse than a pillory to Swift. There was scarcely a bishop in the Church of Ireland or the Church of England for whom Swift did not feel intellectual contempt. In his essay on the Fates of Clergymen, contrasting the neglected genius with the promoted dullard, he has displayed the bitterness of his soul. The least unhappy period of his unhappy life is covered by the Journal to Stella. He was then a leading and dominating figure in a society which has never been surpassed for wit, ease, and charm. How dull the Court was at this time we know from Swift himself. "There was a Drawing-room to-day," he writes to Stella on the 8th of August, 1711, "but so few company that the Queen sent for us into her bedchamber, where we made our bows, and stood about twenty of us round the room while she looked at us round with her fan in her mouth, and once a minute said about three words to some that were nearest her, and then she was told dinner was ready, and went out." Very different was the company which Swift habitually kept. It had its seamy side. There was, for instance, Mrs. Manley, author of a scandalous book called the New Atlantis, and a woman of notorious character, whom he was not ashamed to employ in the work of libelling Whigs. But on the other hand there were Addison, Prior, St. John, Congreve, Arbulhnot, and Pope. "I think Mr. St. John," he wrote to Stella, "the greatest young man I ever knew; wit, capacity, beauty, quickness of apprehension, good learning, and an excellent taste; the best orator in the House of Commons, admirable conversation, good nature, and good manners; generous, and a despiser of money." Beauty is an odd constituent in masculine greatness, and Swift goes on to say that he will not answer for this paragon's sincerity. But otherwise it is a fascinating portrait, and St. John did not, like Alexander, reign alone. Lady Mary Wortley, who knew all the wits, and was an excellent judge, declared that there was no company in the world like Addison's. There was nothing that Swift regretted more in politics than the coolness they made for a time between Addison and him. Arbuthnot, whose racy, humorous style did much to help the negotiations for peace at a pinch, was one of Swift's most intimate friends, and a hundred years after the Tory doctor's death Macaulay wrote: "I love Arbuthnot." Congreve's oral epigrams are said to have been as witty as his comedies, which are wittier than Sheridan's. When Bentley was asked why Pope put him in the Dunciad, he said, "I talked against his Homer, and the portentous cub never forgives." But the portentous cub was never dull, as any one can see who reads his letters. The literary people of those days were sociable in a degree and to an extent which we can hardly understand. In Spence's Anecdotes we read that "Addison's chief companions, before he married Lady Warwick (in 1716), were Steele, Budgell [Eustace Budgell, afterwards a victim of the South Sea Bubble], Philips [Ambrose Philips, author of Pastorals], Carey [Henry Carey, author of Sally in our Alley], Davenant [Charles Davenant, the economist], and Colonel Brett [Henry Brett, M.P.]. He used to breakfast with one or other of them at his lodgings in St. James's Place, dine at taverns with them, then to Button's, and then to some tavern again for supper in the evening: and this was then the usual round of his life." In another anecdote, Pope says that Addison studied all the morning, and then dined at Button's, where in his own little senate he made laws, and sat attentive to his own applause. Button was his own servant, whom he established at a coffee house in Russell Street, opposite the defunct Will's, which is sacred to the memory of Dryden. Steele's idolatrous veneration for Addison, who sometimes played a little on him, excited kindly mirth. But most of us wish we had had the chance of showing it. Addison was the most characteristic genius of that age, for Swift belongs to no age in particular, and Marlborough was simple efficiency idealized. There are no mysterious depths in Addison's thought, and no unapproachable heights in his style. His refined scholarship, his delicate humour, his dignified courtesy, his exquisite breeding, his simple piety, and his unwillingness to give pain, make up the characteristics of a Christian gentleman. The absence of enthusiasm and the predominance of reason fix a type which was not superseded as an object of imitation for seventy years after his death.

CHAPTER IV: SOCIETY AND MANNERS

During Queen Anne's childhood at St. James's Palace, the society of the Court, and of fashionable London, was in the full swing of reaction against the Puritan strictness of the Commonwealth. Never before, and never since, not even under the Regency or in the reign of George the Fourth, has either the stage or the world of fashion been so openly licentious and profane. With a few exceptions, such as Bishop Ken, who did not, however, become a bishop until Anne was nineteen, the Church of England made no protest against vice in high places. The Church had regained its position of ascendency, the King had his own again, besides a good deal that was not his own, and all was well. Anne's secluded life and careful education kept her out of harm's way. Mrs. Barry, who first appeared on the stage under Rochester's patronage when the Princess was a child of eight, taught Her Royal Highness the use of her voice in public, and taught that exceedingly well. Anne's other links with the world were Sarah Jennings, and John Sheffield, Earl of Mulgrave, afterwards Duke of Buckingham, who made premature love to her, and was banished from the Court for so doing by Charles the Second, when she was a girl of seventeen. Her marriage with Prince George of Hanover, the future George the First, had been proposed and rejected a year before. A year later she was actually married to a still duller George, and her long series of misfortunes began. Throughout the years of her maidenhood the rule of the sinners, which superseded the rule of the saints, continued, and she had been a wife for two years when her gloomy father, who atoned for the excesses of his youth by an equally selfish austerity of devotion, removed his brother's friends from Whitehall. Five years before her own wedding she had been introduced to Sarah's husband, John Churchill, whose sister had been the mistress of her own father, and who had himself been distinguished by another royal favourite, Barbara Villiers, Countess of Castlemaine, and Duchess of Cleveland. The only charge ever made against Anne herself was a love of brandy, and that rests upon Jacobite malice. But the moral tone of the society in which she lived was about as low as it could be. The standard of public and private virtue was on a par. The policy of the Cabal, and the Comedies of Dryden, are a pretty good counterpart the one to the other. Charles the Second acted a lie whenever he went to Church, and it was only fear of the priests that checked the dull licentiousness of James. That the Princess Mary and the Princess Anne should have grown up modest and innocent in such surroundings is wonderful. They both made excellent wives, though one was married to a great man, and the other to a mere fool. But, whereas Mary was true to the husband she idolized even when he was not faithful to her, and had a singularly amiable temper, the effect upon her sister of the examples she saw was to plant in her mind the seeds of suspicion and distrust. She lost her mother, Anne Hyde, a woman of blameless character, when she was only six years old, and difference of religion was an insuperable barrier to all intimacy with her young stepmother, Mary of Modena. Her only real friend of her own sex in youth, Sarah Jennings, was a type of the woman fostered by the Restoration, save in the one matter of conjugal fidelity, for which she indemnified herself by scolding and storming at her illustrious husband. Although she chose to call herself a Whig, Sarah's real politics were avarice, pride, and the advancement of her own family at the public expense. To suppose her imbued with the principles of Locke and Somers would be ridiculous. If she had any reason for being a Whig, it was that she hated the Church, and it was probably she who imbued Anne with the notion that the Whigs were enemies of that institution. What exactly it was that Anne meant by the Church cannot easily be ascertained. She was, and Sarah was not, a religious woman. But to call the Church of the Restoration a religious body is to strain a point. The Whigs of the Revolution were Erastians. They were in favour of the ecclesiastical Establishment. They were willing to let its proctors sit in Convocation, and its bishops attend the House of Lords. They merely insisted on Dogberry's principle, "if two men ride on a horse, one must ride behind," that the Church should be servant, and the State should be master. It is not to be supposed that Anne ever formulated to herself the reverse of this proposition. It is more likely that she regarded the Church as the one safeguard against moral evils with which she had been brought into such early contact. During the short reign of her father, however, the Church of England appeared as the champion of popular liberties, which happened for the nonce to coincide with its own. The seven bishops whom James prosecuted for not reading the illegal declaration of independence were the idols of the people, and their acquittal was the signal of his downfall. William's accession produced a change, and indeed a reversal of parts. Five of the seven bishops, including Sancroft and Ken, refused allegiance to a sovereign who did not reign by divine right, and these non-jurors were deprived of their sees. The abusive language in which Anne wrote of William may have been partly due to his conflict with the High Churchmen, and it certainly brought her into serious disfavour with Queen Mary. Whoever offended Mary offended William ten times more. For the remainder of Mary's life, the Princess Anne was made to feel herself in disgrace by the withdrawal of official homage to her rank, and by the dismissal of her friends the Churchills from all the offices they held. She accompanied them into their retirement, and remained with them in seclusion until Mary died.

The death of Mary, which completely shattered for a time the adamantine fortitude of William, was due to the most terrible scourge which had afflicted Europe since the black death. Even in these days of vaccination, cleanliness, and sanitary science smallpox is a serious disease. In 1694, and long afterwards, there was no remedy for it known to the medical profession except careful nursing and the strength of the patient. William himself suffered from it, and had been saved by the extraordinary devotion of his friend Bentinck, the first Earl of Portland. Dr. Radcliffe, whose name is immortalized by the magnificent dome of the library at Oxford, was reported to have most skill in curing it. But it often baffled the physician, it was especially fatal to the young, and it permanently disfigured many who survived the attack. Sanitary science hardly existed in Queen Anne's time, and the art of drainage was in a rudimentary stage. Even fine ladies powdered and painted more than they washed. Fresh air in a house was regarded as neither necessary nor wholesome, and baths were considered effeminate. The condition of towns was such as to foster disease even in palaces, and smallpox was so highly contagious that it might be brought to a palace from a cottage. Readers of Esmond will recollect the terror of Lord Castlewood when he discovers that Harry may be a source of infection, and yet Lord Castlewood was a courageous man. Nothing could save Mary, and her death was a turning point in the life of Anne. She was now heir presumptive to the throne. William received her back into favour, and after four years became reconciled to Marlborough. It was her son's death in the year 1700 that made Anne entirely dependent upon Sarah. After that she took to signing herself "your infortunate Morley," and it was indeed the crowning tragedy of the poor lady's sad life. Only six of her seventeen children lived long enough to be called by their names. The little boy whom William made Duke of Gloucester was the single one that attained any development of mind or character. After his loss she became more sullen and moody. She had dismissed the first physician of the age, John Radcliffe, because she disliked his uncourtly manners, and her acquaintance with Dr. Arbuthnot was of more recent date. The death of her father, in 1701, made a considerable, though not a legal, change in the position of Anne. Her succession to the throne depended constitutionally upon the Bill of Rights, and the Act of Settlement. But a large number of Englishmen ceased to be Jacobites on the death of James, because they did not think that the person calling himself Prince of Wales was his son. Anne herself believed for some time in the story of the warming-pan, and some think that she died believing it. In any case it was believed by thousands, and no formal steps were taken, perhaps could be taken, to refute it until it had become an accepted legend. So long as James the Second lived, the credibility of the tale, or the credulity of the public, was immaterial. He, and he alone, could be the lawful sovereign of those who held the divine right of Kings. Many Jacobites were willing to obey William the Third as the Chief Magistrate whom Parliament had chosen to set over them custos regni, as Sancroft called him, King de facto in the language of the text writers, but not de jure. But though they obeyed him, and would have obeyed Anne in her father's lifetime, their consciences would not have allowed them to take the oath of abjuration. The old James gone, and the young James assumed to be spurious, there was no obstacle whatever to Anne's peaceful and legitimate succession. Resentment against the French King for acknowledging the Pretender became doubly strong where it was thought that the child he acknowledged was not the son of King James and his Italian wife.

Thus, when Anne came to the throne, her subjects might conveniently be divided into four classes. There were those who held that she was simply a usurper, and that their lawful ruler was James the Third. They were energetic, but not numerous, and mostly Catholics. Then came a considerable proportion who waited for better times, holding that, for the sake of peace, they might recognize a Parliamentary arrangement of which they did not approve. A third party, who had been Jacobites while the dethroned monarch lived, held the Pretender to be a mere impostor. Lastly, there were the Whigs, who thought that Parliament could do as it pleased, and that Anne's title rested on the sure foundation of two statutes. People who were not politicians were apt to reflect that, after all, their Sovereign was a Stuart and a woman. Her Stuart blood gave her a respectable degree of legitimacy, and the last woman who reigned alone in England had been the greatest of all her Sovereigns. Elizabeth, however, with her many splendid attributes, had one sordid vice. She grudged the payment of money actually due even to the gallant sailors who had destroyed the power of Spain, and made her mistress of the seas. Anne was remarkably liberal. Besides her munificent benefaction to the Church she gave a sixth part of her Civil List, an annual sum of a hundred thousand pounds, to the expenses of the war. Blenheim Palace is estimated to have cost her not less than two hundred thousand sterling; and when she finally dismissed the Duchess of Marlborough, after innumerable provocations, from employment at Court, she paid her old friend without demur the exorbitant demands for pecuniary solace which that unprincipled woman put forward. She spent comparatively little upon herself, and never bought a jewel during her reign. She would not even purchase the famous diamond brought home from Madras by Governor Pitt, Lord Chatham's grandfather, and sold after her death to the Regent Orleans for about one fourth of its market value. Until they quarrelled about matters unconnected with money, she was a monarch after Godolphin's own heart. The popular phrase "good Queen Anne" had a very different meaning from the once equally popular "good Queen Bess." The public knew little or nothing of Anne's sullen disposition, of the resentment which grew from continual brooding over injuries and slights. They saw that, when the Duchess of Marlborough lost her only son from the prevalent scourge, the Queen showed her the affectionate sympathy of a mother still more cruelly bereaved. They felt the subsequent ingratitude of the Duchess to be without excuse. They perceived that Marlborough, though he had destroyed the tyranny of France, might have become a dangerous dictator himself, if the Queen had granted his request, and made him Captain General for life. They respected Anne for her blameless conduct as a wife, and for her steady devotion to the Church which had attained the highest measure of its popularity by resisting the unconstitutional despotism of her father. To the dry philosophic Calvinism of William the Church of England was only a shade less repugnant than the Church of Rome. Queen Anne loved the Church of her baptism, and showed, so far as she could, most favour to those clergymen who held its claims the highest. She hated Dissenters; and Dissenters were not popular in her reign, when even to profess religious tolerance was to incur the reproach of schism, and the suspicion of infidelity.

Anne had none of the personal dignity which belonged, at least in public, to Elizabeth. Her wretched health was not favourable to the preservation of queenly pomp, and her courtiers often saw her in circumstances of ignominious helplessness. Even strangers were sometimes admitted to curious scenes. Sir John Clerk of Penicuik has left in his Memoirs a quaint description of royalty at Kensington in 1704. Sir John was a supporter of the Union with Scotland, which the Queen had much at heart, and while that measure was preparing, he was admitted to the private apartments, through his patron the Duke of Queensberry. "One day," he says, not in the spirit of a courtier, or perhaps of a gentleman, "one day I had occasion to observe the calamities which attend human nature, even in the greatest dignities of life. Her Majesty was labouring under a fit of gout, and in extreme pain and agony, and on this occasion everything about her was much in the same disorder as about the meanest of her subjects. Her face, which was red and spotted, was rendered something frightful by her negligent dress, and the foot affected was tied up with a pultis and some nasty bandages. I was much affected at this sight, and the more when she had occasion to mention her people of Scotland, which she did frequently to the Duke. What are you, poor mean-like mortal, thought I, who talks in the style of a Sovereign?" More interesting, because less trite, is the account given by the same writer, of a second interview with the Queen two years later, when the Union had been successfully accomplished, with the earnest encouragement and assistance of Anne herself. On this occasion Clerk kissed hands on his appointment to be a Baron of the Exchequer in Scotland. "I cannot remember this incident," he adds, "without making this reflexion, as I have done before that, tho' this great Queen had in her short reign, I mean to the year I saw her, made a very glorious figure in Europe by her armies and fleets abroad, and even in bringing about the Union of the two Kingdoms, which could never be accomplished by any of her predecessors, tho' she was in all respects arbitrix of peace and war in Europe, and by her sovereign authority held the Balance of Power in her hands, yet at the time I was introduced to her to receive her commands for Scotland, she appeared to me the most despicable mortal I had ever seen in any station. The poor lady, as I saw her twice before, was again under a severe fit of the gout, ill-dressed, blotted in her countenance, and surrounded with plasters, cataplasims (sic), and dirty little rags. The extremity of her pain was not then upon her, and it diverted her a little to see company with whom she was not to use ceremonies, otherways I had not been allowed access to her. However, I believe she was not displeased to see anybody, for no Court Attenders ever came near her. All the Incense and adoration offered at Courts were to her Ministers, particularly the Earl of Godolphin, her chief Minister, and the two Secretaries of State; her palace of Kensington, where she commonly resided, was a perfect solitude, as I had occasion to observe several times. I never saw anybody attending there but some of her Guards in the outer Rooms, with one at most (sic) of the Gentlemen of her Bedchamber. Her frequent fits of sickness and the distance of the place from London, did not admit of what are commonly called Drawing-Room nights, so that I had many occasions to think, that few Houses in England belonging to persons of quality were kept in a more private way than the Queen's Royal Palace of Kensington." It must be remembered that Kensington was then a village of gravel pits, with one handsome square before the palace, far beyond the limits of London, though a not unfashionable resort for Londoners in search of fresh air. Swift, however, when he was at Windsor in 1711, drew a different and much more agreeable picture. Among many references to the Queen's love of hunting and sport, he writes: "Mr. Vice Chamberlain lent me his horse to ride about arid see the country this morning. Dr. Arbuthnot, the Queen's physician and favourite, went out with me to the places: we went a little after the Queen and overtook Miss Forester, a maid of honour on her palfrey talking the air; we made her go along with us. We saw a place they have made for a famous horse-race to-morrow, where the Queen will come. We met the Queen coming back and Miss Forester stood like us with her hat off while the Queen went by. ... I was tired with riding a trotting mettlesome horse a dozen miles, having not been on horseback this twelvemonth. And Miss Forester did not make it easier; she is a silly true maid of honour and I did not like her although she be a toast and was dressed like a man."

Anne's influence upon the society of her time, wholesome so far as it went, was small. She discouraged open licentiousness, though she could not exclude Bolingbroke entirely from her counsels, and she loathed the ribaldry even of so great a humorist as Swift, though she could not prevent the Duke of Ormond as Lord Lieutenant of Ireland from making him a dean. It would have been impossible for any woman, and even for any man, between 1712 and 1714, to check duelling, drunkenness, or gambling. A gentleman insulted by a bully in his own rank of society had then no choice but to fight. Even Parliament was not a protection, and the

Duke of Marlborough, after all his victories had been won, invited a blackguard peer who had affronted him in debate to "take the air in the country." This particular encounter did not ensue, because the bully was also a coward. But duels were almost of daily occurrence, and were not uncommonly fatal. They were fought at Hampstead, at Paddington, in Bloomsbury, even in Hyde Park, and it was never thought necessary to leave England for the purpose. Yet by the English law, then and always, duelling was criminal, and to kill a man in a duel was murder, even though the party who lost his life were the party who sent the challenge. That no jury would in the eighteenth century have convicted of a capital crime a man who had fought according to the rules is doubtless true. The utmost the Crown could hope was a verdict of manslaughter, and the sentence would have been a light one. Nevertheless duelling is a singular instance of public opinion brought round by degrees to the law, not, as usually happens, of the law moulded in accordance with public opinion.

Duelling was fostered by drunkenness, and the age of Anne was emphatically drunken. It would be difficult to mention a single man in public life who was habitually sober, except Marlborough, who depended upon the clearness of his head. Swift, who was a dean, and Atterbury, who was a bishop. The fashionable dinner-hour was five, which allowed plenty of lime for steady soaking, and for suppers, when bottles could again be opened. Burgundy was being gradually superseded by port in the later years of the reign. Claret and sweet champagne were also coming into vogue. Immense quantities of ale, home-brewed October, were consumed in the country. In towns the most popular drink was gin, but there was a considerable demand for the more salutary cider. Many men, like Harley, were scarcely sober before they began to drink again. Their habits made them prematurely old, and apoplexy or paralysis carried them off in middle life. Gout was almost universal, and stone, which required a surgical operation without anaesthetics, was very common. A drinking bout sometimes ended in a murderous quarrel, and sometimes in what was called death from natural causes. Societies for the promotion of temperance would have been regarded as insane, and the law rather encouraged than checked the consumption of excisable liquor. When gentlemen began seriously to drink, ladies retired. But a man under the influence of wine must have been one of the first sights to which a girl entering society became accustomed. It was perhaps partly for that reason that girls had very little freedom, and were seldom allowed to leave the house unaccompanied by some sort of duenna. On the other hand, men were at great pains to dress well, their behaviour was ceremonious, and their compliments to the other sex elaborate. They had almost as wide a range of choice as women in the selection of costumes, and if their wigs partly concealed their faces, their knee-breeches set off their legs. The sword was even more essential than the wig, in days when every man might at any moment be required to defend himself or his lady companion. A knowledge of fencing was part of every gentleman's education, and even in the streets of London it was not safe to rely upon the forces of the law. The streets were dimly lighted with oil lamps. The constables were seldom nimble-minded, and not always able-bodied. They had not altered very much since Shakespeare's time, and were far more afraid of the Mohawks than the Mohawks were of them. These Mohawks, or Hawcubites, excited terror in 1712, and gave rise to much the same kind of panic as the garrotters established in London a hundred and fifty years later. But they belonged to a very different order of society. They were young bloods and men about town who, from mere insolence and brutality, attacked foot passengers of both sexes, beat them and cut their noses. The rage of faction attributed their exploits, without a particle of evidence, to a Whig conspiracy, and Swift was so much alarmed by them that, despite his habitual parsimony, he took to hiring chairs. The importance of these particular savages has been exaggerated by historians. They were a transient, though embarrassing, phenomenon, a phase of the lawless roystering which had never really ceased since the Restoration. When it reached scandalous proportions, the soldiers were called out, and the sight of red coats had an immediate effect. The true significance of the Mohawks is that they symbolize the barbarous cruelty which underlay the ceremonious manners of the age. The law itself was cruel. For small offences culprits were still whipped, or burned in the hand. All felonies, from grand larceny, or stealing goods worth two pounds, up to murder, were alike capital. The judicial Bench had vastly improved since the Revolution, and prisoners were no longer browbeaten by the Judges. But they were not allowed Counsel in cases of felony other than treason, and the indictment, being in Latin, was very seldom within their comprehension. At the Old Bailey trials were conducted by the City Judges with indecent haste, and wretches hanged that jurymen might dine. Flogging in the army and navy was inflicted without restraint. Press-gangs crimped men for service in the fleet without regard to their circumstances or situation. Arrest for debt, which might mean lifelong imprisonment, was so common that bailiffs seized the Russian Ambassador in a London street, and Chief Justice Holt, before whom they were brought, could do nothing to them. The Czar, however, in 1712, was Peter the Great, whose wrath, not unnaturally, knew no bounds, and led to the passing of a statute which exempted foreign diplomatists for the future. Peers and Members of the House of Commons, with their servants, were also protected, so that privilege of Parliament was worth having in the eighteenth century, and did not become absolutely meaningless until all arrest on civil process was abolished in 1869. Humanity in gaols was never thought of, and debtors' prisons were as bad as any. Lunatics were chained and flogged, under the horrible delusion that there was no other safe way of treating them. Cockfighting, bull-baiting, and even bear-baiting, were still fashionable pursuits. Kindness to animals was disregarded as mawkish sentimentalism.

Addison's account of the Tory foxhunter in the Freeholder was written two years after the death of Anne. But the time is too short to signify, and the inimitable portrait of the man would do for any period from the Dutch deliverance to the Hanoverian Succession. That foxhunting implied Toryism, Addison assumes as a matter of course. Whigs attended race-meetings, and ran horses. Wharton, for instance, did both, and usually won. But fox-hunters in Addison's day were all, it seems, friends of passive obedience, and enemies of foreign trade, who considered Whigs to be dogs, whelps, and curs. Witches and Presbyterians Addison's fox-hunter held in equal horror. For the impossible offence of witchcraft was still capital in Anne's reign, and the foxhunter enlarged upon the happiness of the neighbouring county, probably Wiltshire, where there was "scarce a Presbyterian except the bishop." The foxhunter was against all foreign alliances. "Our wooden walls," he said, "are our security, and we may bid defiance to the whole world, especially if they should attack us when the militia is out." He was a logical protectionist, maintaining that foreign trade was the ruin of England. Addison, a free trader before Adam Smith, reminded him that all the ingredients in the punch they were drinking came from abroad except the water. At this point the landlord ran to the rescue, and observed with a humour too Addisonian to be quite in character, that "there was no liquor like a cup of English water provided it had malt enough in it." Foxhunting soon became a national sport and ceased to be identified with passive obedience. But Addison's paper illustrates very well the social condition of the English squires under the last of the Stuarts.

They were ignorant, for there was little education either at school or college, except in the case of those who, from ambition or love of learning, educated themselves. The only tests were theological, and there were no examinations. Travelling was slow, difficult, tedious, and expensive. The squire who was not a Parliament man seldom came even to London. He could not afford it. He knew, as a rule, little more than the labourers on his estate, and had as little desire to rise. England was an agricultural country, exporting corn, importing most of the manufactures she consumed, hardly suspecting the wealth of her coal, and feeding her population from her own resources. There was no overcrowding, and food was cheap. The merchants who did business beyond the seas, like Mr. Walter Shandy, whose trade had been with Turkey, were mostly Whigs, hated rivals of the landed interest. The character of Sir Andrew Freeport in the Spectator is a faithful and sympathetic description of a class to which the commercial prosperity of England is mainly due. The South Sea Company, founded in Queen Anne's reign, came soon afterwards to a disgraceful and calamitous end. The East India Company, which dates from Charles the Second, was gradually rising to the splendid position that might have lasted till our own day if it had not been destroyed by the Indian Mutiny in 1857. So early as 1687 the Directors of that Company, merchant princes in every sense of the word, declared that their will and pleasure was to "establish such a polity of civil and military power, and create and secure such a large revenue as may be the foundation of a large, well grounded, sure English dominion in India for all time to come." Their rivals had been the Portuguese, and were now the French. The Mogul conquest of India was completed by Aurungzebe, whose long reign came to an end in 1707. After his death his empire fell gradually to pieces under incompetent successors, and the Mahrattas who "asked no leave of king or chief," plundered it at their will as they rode through Hindostan. The great Frenchman, Joseph Francois Dupleix, who was to dispute with Clive for the paramount power of India, was yet unknown. The possessions of the English Company, still small, were centred at Fort St. George, in Madras. Their double duty, or at least their two-fold business, was to negotiate for further territory with native rulers, and to protect their valuable monopoly from interloping traders, such as Thomas Pitt, who, however, finally made terms with them, and was for twelve years before 1709 President of Fort St. George. He and other Nabobs "shook the pagoda tree" with more energy than scruple, coming home, if they survived the climate, to found families and buy rotten boroughs, then openly sold in the market by due process of law. Such was the origin of the Indian Empire, and of the British Empire itself. The chief British colonies existing in Queen Anne's time were those of North America, to which Newfoundland was added by the Treaty of Utrecht. They began with the arrival of the Mayflower in 1620. The charters taken from them by James the Second were restored by William the Third, who supported James's ally, William Penn, the illustrious Quaker, in the foundation of Pennsylvania. Canada was still French; and the colonies were regarded with disfavour by the Tory party as focuses of Whig politics and Nonconformist schism. Scotland was looked down upon as a nest of Presbyterian ism, which was as the sin of witchcraft, and Ireland, who would willingly have joined in a union with Great Britain if she could have been assured of religious toleration, even for the Protestant Nonconformists of the north, was treated as a barbarous land, the home of wild Papist rapparees. The ideal of the country party, which ruled the roost from 1710 to 1714, was that good old England should eat English beef, drink English ale, and live on English corn.

In London, which had a population of half a million, then thought stupendously large, coffee was a favourite drink with the well-to-do, and coffee houses were the resort of the people who now frequent clubs. The first number of the Spectator describes a few of these haunts. "Sometimes," says the anonymous writer, "I am seen thrusting my Head into a round of Politicians at Will's, and listening with great Attention to the Narratives that are made in those little Circular Audiences. Sometimes I smoak a Pipe at Child's, and while I seem attentive to nothing but the Postman, overhear the Conversation of every Table in the Room. I appear on Sunday night at St. James's Coffee-house, and sometimes join the little Committee of Politicks in the Inner Room, as one who comes there to hear and improve. My Face is likewise very well known at the Grecian, the Cocoa-Tree, and in the Theatres both of Drury-Lane and the Hay-Market. I have been taken for a Merchant upon the Exchange for above these ten years, and sometimes pass for a Jew in the Assembly of Stock-jobbers at Jonathan's. In short, wherever I see a Cluster of People, I always mix with them, though I never open my Lips but in my own Club."

Of these Clubs the Beefsteak, for actors, is the only one which now survives. The reference in the Spectator is probably to the Kitcat, a Whig Club, founded in 1699. The members of the Kitcat had their portraits painted by Kneller, and it is only in reference to the pictures that we now use the name. Christopher Katt was the pastrycook in Shire Lane over whose shop the club first met, consisting of thirty-nine Members, all attached to the Protestant Succession. Among them were Marlborough, Somerset, Sunderland, Wharton, Halifax, and Somers. Garth, Vanbrugh, and Congreve were the literary stars. Of Congreve and Vanbrugh enough has been said. Sir Samuel Garth, author of a poem called The Dispensary, is better known from Pope's description as

"Garth, the best good Christian he.

Although he know it not."

The mutton-pies of this distinguished society were known as "kitcats." Their toasts, and the inscriptions on their glasses, were still more famous. When Prior was expelled from the Kitcat as a Tory, he assisted St. John to found the Brothers, who began to meet on Thursdays in 1711 "for the improvement of friendship, and the encouragement of letters," as St. John wrote to Lord Orrery. Besides St. John and Prior, Harley, Arbuthnot, "Granville the polite," afterwards Lord Lansdowne, Peterborough, and Swift were Brothers. Bolingbroke's extraordinary reputation with men of his own time, so difficult for posterity to understand, was not due merely to his speeches in Parliament, brilliant as they must have been. There was no Hansard in Queen Anne's days, and it was a breach of privilege to report what it would now be considered almost a breach of privilege to suppress. Electors were not even entitled to know how their representatives voted, and it was not the greatest orators who, like Lord Haversham, edited their own speeches for publication. The mere fact that Members never addressed the public in general, or their constituents in particular, through the newspapers, may have fostered the excellence of debate as such. It is difficult to judge from traditional fragments, or from publications which may have owed much to a subsequent waste of midnight oil. St. John's success in the House of Commons was universally acclaimed so long as he sat there. His talk in the Brothers' Club, and at private dinners, fascinated a far more critical and exacting audience than the merchants, foxhunters, lawyers, and men about town, who sat in St. Stephen's Chapel, between the existing Houses of Parliament and Westminster Hall. Bolingbroke's great effort to use his conversational powers, and his personal magnetism, for a public object was a failure. On the very day of Oxford's dismissal from office, the 27th of July, 1714, he entertained Stanhope, Craggs, Pulteney, and Walpole, all Whigs, at his house in Golden Square. It was only after they had separated without any practical result, and after the project of putting the Treasury into Commission had failed for want of five respectable Commissioners on the Tory side, that Bolingbroke in despair turned to Shrewsbury and begged him to take Oxford's post. But Bolingbroke could dazzle, if he could not persuade. Preeminently clubable, to use Dr. Johnson's word, in a clubable age, he was the life and soul of the Brothers, to whom even Swift considered it an honour to belong. The Brothers were not a Club in our sense of the term. They had no club-house, no newspapers, no library. They dined at different taverns, and were often charged sums which Swift, the sober man among them, considered, not unjustly, to be extortionate. Professing to despise the toasts and merriment of the Kitcat, they met to talk and to drink. They did not gamble. There were gaming houses for those who liked them, and no attempt was made to check a vice which public lotteries under the sanction of the Legislature directly encouraged. The expenses of the war were provided by loans, taxes, and lotteries. But betting, though common enough, was in those days the pursuit of idlers rather than, as it afterwards became, the relaxation of statesmen. Even Godolphin laid most of his wagers at Newmarket, where the races were actually run. As to shutting up those tables which existed, it would have had to be done by the army. The watch, who could not keep the streets in order, nor prevent chairmen in search of a job from levying blackmail upon foot passengers, would have been as unfit for the purpose as Dogberry and Verges themselves. Colley Cibber, who wrote his Apology for his Own Life in the reign of George the Second, says, with a truly insular spirit, "We are so happy as not to have a certain Power among us which, in another country, is called the Police." Better, he thought, endure even disorder in the Playhouse than fly to such a remedy as that.

The position of women in Queen Anne's reign would now be regarded as intolerable. A married woman was the slave of her husband, who could compel her by force to live with him. Marriage was indissoluble, except by Act of Parliament, and no woman could obtain a divorce. All property acquired or earned by a wife, except under settlements, then just becoming known, was the property of her husband, who could squander it without redress in any way he pleased. He might even beat her if he did not use too large and heavy a stick, "reasonable chastisement" being legal in her case, as in her children's. Extreme indulgence to the licentiousness of the male sex was combined with extreme severity to the victims of seduction, especially if their offspring became chargeable upon the parish. On the other hand, a pretty woman in easy circumstances had a very agreeable life while she was single, and a good deal of practical freedom after matrimony had abridged her nominal rights. The art of gallantry has never been more assiduously cultivated than by the beaux of Queen Anne. Amongst the famous toasts of the Kitcat Club was Marlborough's favourite daughter, the Countess of Sunderland, called by her father "the little Whig." Addison has described, as he alone could, the privileges of those fair charmers whom he calls Idols. "The Playhouse," he writes, "is very frequently filled with Idols; several of them are carried in Procession every evening about the Ring, and several of them set up their worship even in Churches. They are to be accosted in the language proper to the Deity. Life and Death are in their Power: Joys of Heaven and Pains of Hell are at their disposal: Paradise is in their Arms, and Eternity in every moment that you are present with them. Raptures, Transports, and Ecstasies are the Rewards which they confer; Sighs and Tears, Prayers and broken Hearts are the Offerings which are paid to them. Their Smiles make men Happy; their Frowns drive them to Despair. I shall only add under this Head, that Ovid's Book of the Art of Love is a kind of Heathen Ritual, which contains all the Forms of Worship which are made use of to an Idol." Then, with a delightful touch of the true Addisonian humour, not lost upon a humorist of our own day, Mr. Anthony Hope, the essayist continues, "I must here observe that those Idolaters who devote themselves to the Idols I am speaking of differ very much from all other kinds of Idolaters. For as others fall out because they worship different Idols, these Idolaters quarrel because they worship the same." The art of flirtation, essentially a feminine art, kept pace with masculine gallantry. The word is derived from the use of the fan, introduced from Spain; for unfurling that banner of the sex comprehends, as the Spectator says, "several little flirts and vibrations," all going to make up the complicated verb to flutter, which might be, as we learn from the same high source, "angry, modest, timorous, confused, merry, or amorous." An academy for training girls in the exercise of the fan was also proposed in the Spectator, and would perhaps have been almost as useful as the few girls' schools of the period. For if the education of boys was sadly imperfect, and if Dr. Busby of Caroline fame was worshipped by Sir Roger, whose grandfather he had flogged, as a distant memory, the education of girls was hardly intellectual at all. They learnt to cook, as only English women would condescend to cook, and to sew. Most of them could read, after a fashion, and a few, a very few, could spell. Fine ladies despised orthography, which, in the absence of etymological research, was become matter of argument, or of guess. Even proper names were variously composed, on principles which may be roughly described as phonetic, according to the taste and fancy of the speller. Some light is thrown by the invaluable Spectator upon what the ladies of 1711 read. There were no novels, except some collections of short stories, such as Mrs. Aphra Behn's, and The Grand Cyrus, translated from the French of Mademoiselle de Scudery, the only book in the lady's library described by Addison which had "a Pin stuck in one of the middle leaves." The Court of Cyrus was the Court of Louis, and his real capital was Versailles. Addison's lady had also an English translation of Malebranche, which does not give a very high idea of her literary accomplishments. For some acquaintance with the French tongue, which Marlborough is said to have known better than his own, was then regarded as essential to an educated woman, just as an educated man could not afford to be ignorant of Latin, unless he was a soldier, however complete might be his lack of science, history, modern languages, and Greek. The lady's copy of Locke on the Human Understanding had a paper of patches in it, which meant, I presume, that she had lost them. The classic authors, on the other hand, were "in wood," while Mrs. Manley's New Atlantis had a key to it. Tom Durfey's Tales in Verse, which cannot have done their owner much good, were "bound in Red Leather gilt on the Back, and doubled down in several Places." The lady had Dryden's Juvenal, which is coarser than Juvenal himself, and somebody else's Virgil, which must have been far inferior to Dryden's. Congreve's Millamant in The Way of the World, perhaps the most fascinating woman of the English drama outside Shakespeare, was doubtless the type of excellence in the younger circles of Queen Anne.

Besides the Duchess of Marlborough and Lady Masham, the most prominent women in the Court of Queen Anne were the Duchess of Somerset and the Duchess of Shrewsbury. Charles Seymour, sixth Duke of Somerset, was appointed Master of the Horse on Queen Anne's accession. He had been civil to Anne as a young Princess, when little notice was taken of her, and continued in her favour until he was dismissed with Marlborough in 1711. He was known as the Proud Duke, though what he had to be proud of history does not disclose. His wife, who was a Percy, the last Earl of Northumberland's daughter, succeeded the Duchess of Marlborough as Mistress of the Robes, and had great influence with the Queen. She remained at Court after the Duke had been turned out, and Swift's impatience to get rid of her is one of the most comical episodes in the Journal to Stella. Her leanings were Whig, and opposed to Lady Masham's, so that the two women were constantly struggling for the poor Queen's soul. Swift called the Duchess a designing woman, because her designs were contrary to his own, and even alarmed him for his personal safety. They did not procure, as he feared they would, the dismissal of Oxford and Bolingbroke. But they were successful so far as she herself was concerned. For she retained her place throughout the reign, and was chief mourner at the Queen's funeral. Queen Anne was a stickler for etiquette, and liked to have a Duchess as Mistress of the Robes. The Duchess of Somerset was, moreover, an English woman, whereas the Duchess of Shrewsbury, though descended in the female line from Robert Dudley, Queen Elizabeth's Earl of Leicester, was an Italian. It was she who first gave Swift the name of Presto, being unable to pronounce his own, and was thought to have "wonderful art in entertaining and diverting people, though she would sometimes exceed the bounds of decency." She was, or thought herself, a Tory, and Lady Cowper, who was a Whig, designates her as "the most cunning, designing woman alive, obliging to people in prosperity, and a great party woman." Unlike her stately husband, a fine gentleman, and a real scholar, she was a lively, agreeable rattle, attractively indiscreet, and much admired by Swift, whose neighbour she became in Ireland when the Duke was Lord Lieutenant. Everybody liked the Duke of Shrewsbury, and nobody trusted him. He had been all things to all men, and was known as the King of Hearts. Yet at the critical moment, in the last days of July 1714, it was Shrewsbury as much as any one man who secured a peaceful succession for the House of Hanover.

The England of Anne was not overpopulated. There were no congested districts, and no factories. The Poor Law dated from the reign of Elizabeth, and justices of the peace had a theoretically unlimited power of charging the rates for the relief of the poor. The population of England was scarcely greater than the population of London is now, and the population of London then was about equal to the population of Oldham at the present time. It was the War of the Spanish Succession which first raised the National Debt to a considerable figure. But the land tax was not augmented, and there was no income tax at all. There were heavy duties on the importation of goods from abroad, partly for revenue, and partly to encourage native industries. The war drained the country of able-bodied men, and no provision had been made for the civil employment of soldiers when the Treaty of Utrecht was signed. Chelsea Hospital had been built for military veterans in the reign of CharlesII; but otherwise those who had been fighting their country's battles for years were left to starve, to beg, to be a burden on the parish, or to swell the ranks of highwaymen, highway robbery being at that time a lucrative pursuit, of which the profits were large, and in which the risks were small.

Defoe, who could not be happy for long without a pen in his hand, conducted during the first decade of the eighteenth century a journal which he called the Review, and of which he wrote the whole, or almost the whole, himself. Although Defoe's political conduct was not wise, and his relations with Harley are very little to his credit, he remained in his published writings staunch to Whig principles and to free trade. He satirized the Jacobites with such successful irony that the Queen took him to be a Jacobite himself, and Harley had solemnly to assure his Sovereign that his facetious friend was joking. He supported the unpopular Treaty with France in 1713, with arguments which Cobden might have applied to the Commercial Treaty of 1860. Against bribery at elections, which there was then nothing to check save public opinion, he declaimed in words of almost brutal indignation. More light, however, is thrown upon the habits of the times by Defoe's curious outburst against begging. "If all the beggars of this nation," he writes, "had a charter to join themselves into a body, they would be the richest corporation in the kingdom. The disease is corroded; the leprosy is on the walls; we are possessed with the begging devil; we have poor without begging, and beggars without poverty. Strange that nature can be depressed to so much meanness, to ask a man's charity for mere covetousness, and stoop to beg without want. How often have we known men that have stood with a broom in their hands to sweep a passage, and beg your alms for God's sake, leave a thousand pounds in gold behind them? Two or three famous instances of this we have had very lately, one of which has left three thousand pounds to a charity." The laws against vagrancy at this time were very severe. But whipping sturdy beggars had about as much effect as hanging highwaymen. It made criminals more desperate without subtracting from their number.

On this subject Addison wrote better, and with more knowledge, than any of his contemporaries. Into the mouth of his Whig merchant. Sir Andrew Freeport, he has put language as sound and plain as any to be found in the Wealth of Nations, which did not appear till 1776. Addison introduces his discourse, which occupies the two hundred and thirty-second number of the Spectator, with his usual simplicity and ease. "The other day," says he, "as soon as we were got into his chariot, two or three Beggars on each side hung upon the Doors, and solicited our Charity with the usual Rhetorick of a sick Wife or Husband at home, three or four helpless little Children, all starving with Cold and Hunger. We were forced to part with some Money to get rid of their Importunity; and then we proceeded on our Journey with the Blessings and Acclamations of these People." Sir Andrew moralizes. What good, he asks, have they done by their generosity? Their healths will be drunk at the next alehouse. They will have promoted the trade of the victualler, and contributed to the excise of the Government. But how much wool have these poor creatures upon their backs? Will they be better dressed next time? No, they must wear rags to excite compassion. "I have often thought," he goes on, "that no Man should be permitted to take Relief from the Parish, or to ask it in the Street, till he has first purchased as much as possible of his own Livelihood by the Labour of his own hands; and then the Publick ought only to be taxed to make good the Deficiency. If this Rule was strictly observed we should see everywhere such a multitude of New Labourers as would in all probability reduce the Prices of all our Manufactures. It is the very Life of Merchandize to buy cheap and sell dear. The Merchant ought to make his Out-Set as cheap as possible that he may find the greater Profit upon his Return, and nothing will enable him to do this like the Reduction of the Price of Labour upon all our Manufactures. This too would be the ready way to increase the number of our Foreign Markets. The Abatement of the Price of the Manufacturer would pay for the Carriage of it to more distant Countries, and this Consequence would be equally beneficial both to the Landed and Trading Interests. As so great an Addition of Labouring Hands would produce this happy Consequence both to the Merchant and the Gentleman, our Liberality to common Beggars and every other Obstruction to the Increase of Labourers, must be equally pernicious to both." After this most sensible exordium, upon which the Charity Organization Society could not well improve, Sir Andrew Freeport proceeds to philosophize upon the division of employments in a style which even Adam Smith has scarcely surpassed. "It is certain," wrote Addison in Sir Andrew's name, "that a single Watch could not be made so cheap in proportion by one only man as a hundred Watches by a hundred, for as there is vast variety in the Work, no one person could equally suit himself to all the Parts of it, the Manufacture would be tedious and at last but clumsily performed. But if an hundred Watches were to be made by a hundred Men, the case may be assigned to one, the Dials to another, the Wheels to another, the Springs to another, and every other part to a proper Artist. As there would be no need of perplexing any one Person with too much Variety, every one would be able to perform his single part with greater Skill and Expedition, and the hundred Watches would be finished in one-fourth Part of the Time of the first one, and every one of them one-fourth Part of the Cost, though the Wages of every man were equal. The Reduction of the Price of the Manufacture would increase the Demand of it, all the same Hands would be still employed, and as well paid. The same Rule will hold in the Cloathing, the Shipping, and all the other Trades whatsoever. And then an Addition of Hands to our Manufactures will only reduce the Price of them, the Labourers will still have as much Wages, and will consequently be enabled to purchase more Conveniences of Life, so that every Interest in the Nation would receive a Benefit from an Increase of our working People." If to be in advance of one's age is to state clearly and prove conclusively propositions universally accepted a hundred years after one's death, Addison is certainly entitled to that praise. But it must not be supposed that Sir Andrew Freeport and his theories are pure creations of the Addisonian fancy. There would have been no point in Sir Andrew, who fills so large a place in the Spectator, if he had not expressed, of course with that curious felicity which was Addison's own, the ideas that prevailed among the better informed members of his own class. Not one man of business in a hundred had then, or has now, any theory of trade at all. He subsists on experience and rule of thumb. Even in the seventeenth century there were exceptions, such as Sir Dudley North, and in the eighteenth century there must have been many more. The most interesting part of Addison's Sir Andrew is that he saw the immense value of foreign trade in promoting native industry. Woollen manufactures owed much, as we have seen, to the Methuen Treaty with Portugal, though unhappily the nature of that instrument precluded a commercial treaty with France in 1713. But it is impossible to conceive Sir Andrew Freeport sympathizing with the ignorant outcry against the linen trade of Ireland, or believing that its restriction, even if just, would help the woollen trade of England. Sir Andrew knew, and therefore Addison knew, that trade was not war, and that if Ireland were a foreign nation instead of part of the Queen's dominions, her prosperity would still be advantageous to Great Britain. The most wholesome feature of life in those days is that so much of it was spent in the open air, not in mines, factories, or workshops. If wages were low, and all combinations to raise them illegal, food was reasonably abundant, and land was plentiful. There were small yeomen, as well as large squires, and copyhold, which is now a nuisance, was then a protection. Poaching was ordinary trespass, not punishable as a crime, though man-traps and spring guns were set by the cruel for the unwary, and justices of the peace, if we may believe Fielding, who wrote in the middle of the century with his eye on the beginning, did not always confine their jurisdiction within the limits of the law. Game, however, was by no means strictly preserved, and the lives of men were not sacrificed to fur or feathers. Sheep-stealing was the great crime in the country, as shop-lifting was the great crime in the town, both being capital, partly on the ground that they were difficult to detect. When manslaughter was not an offence for which a man could be hanged, and larceny was, the law might fairly be said to regard property as more sacred than life. But indeed the Parliaments of Queen Anne were more concerned with the extirpation of heresy than with the amendment of criminal jurisprudence. Latitudinarian divines of the establishment, such as Clarke and Hoadly, were safe enough. Catholics were Jacobites, and could not be really patriots. To give them votes would have been like giving arms to rebels. Nonconformists, on the other hand, acknowledged a Parliamentary title to the throne, and were the most zealous champions of the Protestant Succession. To persecute them was as foolish as it was unjust, though it can scarcely be said to have been unpopular, for the rigid rule of the Commonwealth was still remembered. Baptists, Congregationalists, and Presbyterians were then the principal bodies of Protestant Dissenters. Presbyterians were perhaps the most offensive to militant High Churchmen, because they were the dominant Church in Scotland, and sat in both Houses of the British Parliament. When the enemies of Bishop Burnet had exhausted all other terms of abuse, they called him a Presbyterian, although he had done his best to save the victims of Oates and Dangerfield. The exhibition of militant and aggressive High Churchmanship at the close of Queen Anne's reign was not accompanied by any spiritual movement in the Church itself. The Queen herself was indeed truly pious. So, in a different way, was Burnet. Swift and Atterbury were ecclesiastical politicians, hating Dissenters and Whigs, and so fulfilling the law of Christ. Their triumph, however, was short, for the pace was too good to last. It cannot be said of the Whigs in those days that they were friends of Protestant Dissenters or honest champions of religious toleration. They used Nonconformity for their own purposes, and did not hesitate to throw the Nonconformist over when they had done with him, as the Occasional Conformity Act is enough to show. Between such a man as Lord Wharton, and such a man as Dr. Watts, there could be no community of motive or of aim. Bishop Burnet approached more nearly than any other Whig or Churchman of his day to the modern idea of religious equality. But Burnet's first wife had been an ardent Presbyterian, and he was freely charged by High Churchmen, as Archbishop Tait was in the succeeding century, with being a Presbyterian himself. To Bishop Atterbury, a courageous man, whose private character was beyond reproach, the heresy and schism of Presbyterians and Congregationalists were more offensive than the ribaldry of Swift or the immorality of Bolingbroke. While the Queen, unassisted by any of her Ministers, laboured for the spread of religion through the Church, the Church itself, at least as represented by Convocation, was absorbed in bitter ecclesiastical disputes. Addison's jovial innkeeper was under the especial patronage of the Tory foxhunting squire because though he seldom went to church, he had taken part in pulling down several chapels. Atterbury's eloquent and ostentatious zeal for the Church of England did not prevent him from doing his best to violate the Act of Settlement, by setting up a sovereign who was devoted to the Church of Rome. The Jacobite Catholics, including almost every Catholic except Pope, did work, whatever may be thought of their methods, for the cause of a religion in which they sincerely believed. Being forbidden to take an open part in politics, they were exempt from many of the temptations which beset the practical politician. It was their misfortune as much as their fault that their interests were not the interests of the nation, and that they could hardly be patriots, except in Ireland.

Froude has expressed the opinion, for which there is much to be said, that an Act of Union between Great Britain and Ireland should have immediately followed the union between England and Scotland in 1707. So early as the 4th of October, 1703, the Duke of Ormond, then Viceroy of Ireland, wrote to an English Secretary of State, Lord Nottingham, and told him that the Irish House of Commons, which was exclusively Protestant, "considering the many misfortunes the country lay under in point of trade," desired a union. The reference is to the unjust and unwise legislation of William which, treating Ireland as a foreign country, prohibited the import of Irish woollens to the English market. That this protective measure injured England as well as Ireland few, if any, statesmen of that age were enlightened enough to see. English Ministers, such as Godolphin, did make an honest effort to right the balance, not of trade but of justice, by fostering and extending the encouragement granted to the manufacture of Irish linen by a statute of Charles the Second. The project of a Union between England and Ireland, though earnestly supported by the Irish Chancellor, Sir Richard Cox, was quietly allowed to drop. The difficulties were enormous. Cox was a staunch Protestant, who had adhered at the Revolution to William of Orange, and had been present at the battle of the Boyne. He would have regarded Catholic emancipation as madness, as equivalent to making the Pretender a gift of Ireland. The Penal Laws were in full force, and no one in authority dreamt of consulting the Catholic population, inside or outside the Pale. They were as politically dumb as the people of India are to-day. The Presbyterians of the North, of the Ulster Plantation, were a much more serious obstacle to Union from the English Churchman's point of view. The Irish Church was the Church of a small minority, but it monopolized political power. If men unfit to be bishops anywhere were appointed to English sees, the Irish sees were sometimes filled by men whom no Minister would have set over an English diocese. Most clergymen of the Irish Church, including Swift, would have fought hard against any relaxation of the tests imposed upon Presbyterians. Even the union with Scotland would hardly have been carried without the personal influence of the Queen, and there is no evidence that Anne cared anything for Ireland. Scottish Jacobitism was dangerous. Irish Jacobitism was impotent, a quantity that could be neglected in the problem of government. Regarding political, or even commercial, union as impossible, Godolphin turned his mind to the improvement of the linen trade, which owed much of its progress in Ulster to the skill and enterprise of Louis Crommelin, a French refugee. It was proposed to remove Crommelin, if he would go, further south, and assist him in establishing a linen manufactory at Kilkenny, the most central place in the three provinces of Munster, Leinster, and Connaught. The argument for use in England was that the spread of the linen trade on one side of St. George's Channel would promote a corresponding growth of the woollen trade on the other. But the English merchant of 1706, when this scheme was broached, firmly held that the prosperity of one country must be detrimental to another, and the erection of the Linen Hall in Belfast made him think that this particular business was becoming too successful. In vain was he assured that no boon would be bestowed upon the "mere Irish;" that the English of the Pale or the Scotsmen of Ulster would get it all. He was afraid of any interference with the importation of linen from Germany, Holland, and Flanders. So nothing could be done to spread the manufacture, and the Linen Board, a body of trustees created by Royal Warrant in 1707, confined its operations to Ulster, with results that have profoundly affected the history of Ireland from that day to this. The Penal Laws of Anne require no epithet. A bare statement of them is enough. By an Act of 1703 a Catholic was forbidden to be the guardian of his own children, or to disinherit a Protestant child. A Catholic could not purchase real property, nor take a lease for more than thirty years, nor succeed to an estate held by a Protestant. Another Act, passed in 1709, compelled a Catholic father to support any of his children who became Protestants, and gave rewards to informers against unregistered priests. Cruel as these laws were, it does not appear that in Anne's reign they were rigorously enforced. For one thing, Irish Protestants were not united. An Irish Churchman did not regard a Presbyterian as a Churchman at all. He could not deny that title to a Catholic without impeaching the validity of his own orders. For another thing, public opinion, even when most hostile to Catholic emancipation, was not in favour of the penal laws, and it would have required a whole country-side of informers to carry them out in full. Catholic land-owners had Protestant friends who were willing to help them by legal subterfuges, and in Ireland the person of a priest has always been sacred to the people. Throughout the eighteenth century Irish hatred of England grew, until at length it became really formidable. During the War of the Succession Irishmen were eager to fight for France. But in Ireland itself the Boyne and Aughrim had crushed out all danger of rebellion.

If any age in English history can be described as one of temperate felicity, it is probably that which followed the Treaty of Utrecht. Twelve years of war had not raised taxation to an oppressive level, nor the debt to an alarming height. Pope and Swift, Addison and Steele, were opening a new and rich mine of literature, as various as it was full and deep. The Spectator contained the germ of the English novel, destined in a few years to supplant for ever translations from Mademoiselle de Scudery, and Tom Durfey, and Mrs. Aphra Behn. That the Daily Courant would develop into the modern Press was then as little foreseen as that Daniel Defoe, the political reviewer and pamphleteer, would write the best story of adventure in the English language. India was already a source of profit, and not yet a cause of anxiety. The American colonies traded peaceably with their metropolis, and gave no trouble. France was crushed, Spain was contented; the Holy Roman Empire, neither holy Roman nor imperial, had received a new lease of its harmless, tolerant, unaggressive existence. At home there was no surplus population, no chronic want of employment, no poverty that could not be relieved. Competition had hardly set in. Although the land laws were bad, and the criminal law was worse, the squire joined his tenants in sport, and juries gave a kind of informal protection against the worst barbarities of the statute-book. Judges who would have fainted at the thought of abolishing capital punishment for felony took care that it should not always be carried out, and in the absence of counsel for the prisoners were often the best check upon the prosecution. Wool was woven and coal was dug by primitive methods, but under healthy conditions. If there was not much cricket or football, there was abundance of fishing, hunting, shooting, and coursing, without undue preservation of fish or of game. The low standard of public morals, the excessive gallantry of the fashionable class, did not affect the private lives and conduct of humble folk. If the spirit of enterprise was defective, a spirit of satisfaction was pretty generally diffused. The great cause of material misery, the pressure of population upon means of subsistence, had not begun to work. There were vast tracts of open space, even near London, which nobody cared to occupy, and where even highwaymen were seldom disturbed. Highwaymen were the terror of the rich, or at least of the well-to-do. The common people heeded them not at all. Popular education, in day schools or in Sunday schools, there was none. Even reading, writing, and arithmetic were luxuries of the upper and middle classes. The lower orders were told by the clergy, themselves at that time an obsequious race, to obey their betters, meaning those who were better off than themselves. On the other hand, there was no fierce struggle for life, no disappointment with the fruits of ambitious training, no cities overcrowded, no professions overstocked. Landlords could always let their farms, but they could not let them at exorbitant rents that would not pay. Domestic servants were numerous, but they could not be had for starvation wages. There was no sweating. Apprenticeship meant duties on the part of the master, as well as on the part of the servant. The spirit of democracy was unborn in England, though the Presbyterian system fostered it in Scotland, and it had been taken to the American colonies by the Nonconformist victims of religious or irreligious persecution at home. William Penn, the most distinguished member of the Society of Friends, a man of singularly beautiful character, deeply and sincerely Christian, was nevertheless a fine gentleman and a courtier. Penn was a human being, and therefore not always consistent. But the serious charges made against him on plausible evidence by Macaulay have broken down on further investigation, and resolve themselves into ai strange case of mistaken identity. He used his influence with successive monarchs on behalf of his own community, whether in England or in America, and of complete toleration for all sects. Catholics included. He was no more a democrat than Isaac Watts. The Quakers, though they did not acknowledge titles, or any distinctions of social rank, were averse from political as from other quarrels, and determined to live peaceably with all men. Among Queen Anne's statesmen the one professed republican was the Earl of Sunderland, son-in-law of the first, and father of the second, Duke of Marlborough. Sunderland affected to call himself Charles Spencer, and expressed a hope that he should survive the peerage. The Queen was shocked. Those who knew him better smiled; for in an age of intrigue there were few such astute intriguers, and he passed his whole life in courts. Whigs were indeed even less democratic than Tories, and more remote from the people. It was their design to govern in the name of the sovereign, and because they had also the capacity, they succeeded. Circumstances favoured them. A second, or even a long-lived William of Orange would have been fatal to their plans. A Queen of less than average ability with a perfect nonentity for her husband, was the precise combination they required. Their temporary failure in 1710 was due to their own mismanagement, and to the Duchess of Marlborough's temper. In 1714 the stars in their courses fought against Oxford and Bolingbroke. Even Wharton might have seen the finger of Providence in the sudden death of Queen Anne. The quiet and almost undisputed succession of George the First has been called the greatest miracle in English history. There is no miraculous element in it. What might have happened at the General Election of 1714 if a democratic suffrage had prevailed must always be doubtful. Happily for the Whigs and for the Protestant cause, trade was prosperous, and the mercantile community believed that their business would be threatened by a disputed succession. The Whigs had seized power while Anne was dying, and in power they were left. How little they could trust even such constituent bodies as then existed the Septennial Act of 1716 is enough to prove. They had no belief in the people. They believed in a ruling aristocracy, in themselves. They were not unwilling that this privileged class should from time to time be recruited from new men, such as Somers, Cowper, and Walpole. Their habit of marrying untitled heiresses prevented them from becoming a caste, and they had a genuine zeal for personal freedom. But the idea of the people governing themselves, through their representatives, or at all, was to them not even a dream. It was Utopianism or, in plain English midsummer madness. The principles of 1688 were to Englishmen then what the principles of 1789 are to Frenchmen now. As there are French Royalists now, so there were English, and still more Scottish, Jacobites then. But the bulk of the upper and middle classes, the vocal part of the nation, were loyal to the Act of Settlement as the sequel of the Bill of Rights.

The hopes of the Jacobites, revived by the death of William, were destroyed by the death of Anne. They could no longer rely upon France, and Ireland outside the English Pale was politically dead. Exclusion of Catholics from all power in the State was sure to be strengthened rather than weakened by any rising on behalf of the Pretender. The Union with Scotland was denationalizing the Lowlands, and the Highlands were the one dangerous part of Anne's three kingdoms. To be a Jacobite in Great Britain under the first two Hanoverian Kings was to risk not merely political position, but also life and estate. Impeachment was still a regular constitutional process, conviction involved forfeiture, at least in England, and capital punishment for treason was inflicted without scruple. There was no possibility of a British Sovereign. The choice lay between a German and a Frenchman; a German in possession and a Frenchman in exile. Moreover the man in possession was a Protestant, and the refugee was a Catholic. The Act of Settlement had been acknowledged by the Treaty of Utrecht. Louis the Fourteenth would as soon fight the Duke of Marlborough single-handed as go to war again. Few Englishmen had seen the Pretender, and most Englishmen knew that he had fought against England when the Hanoverians fought on her side. No promises or guarantees of religious liberty that he might give, could be stronger than those which his father had broken. The Elector of Hanover would be King by Act of Parliament, and would not violate the Constitution unless he were mad. The greatest musician and the greatest painter in England were Germans. Even Marlborough could not have beaten France so thoroughly without German aid. Scarcely any one in England at that time thought of learning German, for there was not supposed to be any German literature, and educated Germans could speak French. The Empire, however, had become by custom hereditary in the House of Hapsburg; the head of the

Hohenzollerns had been crowned King of Prussia; and though Germany was still a geographical expression, the Emperor controlled the balance of power in Europe. That Britain, having been annexed to Holland, had now been appropriated by Hanover, was a good point for Jacobites. But it was under a Stuart Prince who reigned by right divine that the Dutch cannon were heard in Fleet Street as Dutch ships sailed up the Thames.

The wife of Lord Chancellor Cowper, who abolished the scandalous habit of taking annual presents from the counsel practising before him, has left in her Diary a striking description of the country between Hampton Court and London. Lady Cowper, an extremely clever, and a highly accomplished woman, wrote her journal at the beginning of George the First's reign, when she was waiting upon the future Queen Caroline, then Princess of Wales. Although the date of the following entry is the 28th of October, 1716, it may be fairly applied to the England which Queen Anne left, the England of Uncle Toby and Corporal Trim. At that autumnal season the Prince's Court left their suburban, then their rural, retreat for their town house in Leicester Fields. "The day," says Lady Cowper, "was wonderfully fine and nothing in the world could be pleasanter than the Passage," made in a barge, "nor give one a better idea of the Riches and Happiness of this Kingdom." Although courtiers seldom see the less agreeable part of life, Lady Cowper's observation is confirmed from other sources, and trustworthy evidence paints this period as one of the brightest in our annals. The two chief drawbacks were the highwaymen and the beggars. Even Lady Cowper speaks of footpads, "pads" as they were then familiarly called, in Bedford Row, and refers to her security at Kensington when soldiers were camping in Hyde Park, as "one might come from London any time of the Night without Danger."

The age of Anne, great in politics, in literature, and in war, was not very fruitful in scientific discoveries. The looms which made its excellent broadcloth were worked by hand. Coal was brought from mines by men and horses. A mechanical method of raising water had been devised at the close of the seventeenth century by Thomas Savery, the inventor of paddle-wheels. But it was not altogether successful, until in 1698 Savery took into partnership an ingenious blacksmith from Dartmouth called Thomas Newcomen. Newcomen's pumping-engine, which remained in use for the greater part of the eighteenth century, was equivalent in power to five horses and a half. From a depth of a hundred and fifty-six feet it could raise fifty gallons of water in a minute. Humble as such an achievement must seem now, it had much public utility then. Newcomen's was a kind of atmospheric steam-engine, which obtained its motive force by exhausting the air from a cylinder that had been provided with a piston. Savery 's steam-engine scarcely deserves to be called an anticipation of Watt's. But according to Mr. Ashton's Social Life in the Reign of Queen Anne it "was as ingenious as it was simple. Two boilers with furnaces supplied the steam. This was admitted alternately by means of a handle worked by man or boy, into one of two elliptical receivers, where it condensed, formed a vacuum and the water rushed in and filled its place. When full the application of steam ejected it from the receiver, and forced it up the pipe, and so de novo." This was an ingenious device, no doubt, but it cannot be called a simple application of the propelling power of steam.

Travelling in Queen Anne's reign was difficult, uncomfortable, and even dangerous. The danger, as has been said, was from highway robbery, which flourished almost unchecked. Roads were bad, and a traveller from London to Bath, about the year 1710, describes the last part of the road, after Chippenham, as more perilous than the Alps. The time was two days, and the fare sixteen shillings. Stage coaches ran to most towns, and traffic was conducted by packhorses, waggons, or canals. There were plenty of post-houses, and postmasters were bound by their license to provide horses at a fixed tariff, with guides, for riding or driving. In London there were at this time eight hundred hackney carriages, the fare being fixed at eighteen pence a mile. A more fashionable conveyance was the sedan-chair. There were three hundred licensed chairs in London, the fixed charge being one shilling a mile, though a gratuity was always demanded by the chairmen, notorious bullies and cheats. Six horses with postillions were usual for the coaches of the rich, wealth without ostentation being even rarer in the days of Anne than it is now. Eight thousand pounds was the price of the chair which Queen Anne gave to the first King of Prussia in 1709. Letters were taken out of London three days a week by mail-coaches. Before 1711, there was a penny post for London, and a twopenny post for the country, established by William Dockwra in 1684. The Duke of York as Postmaster General obtained a prohibition of Dockwra's enterprise as an infringement of his own monopoly, and in 1711 the penny post was abolished. Correspondence became expensive and rare, except for those who could find Members of Parliament to frank their letters. Private competition was rigorously suppressed, and the public meekly acquiesced in the sacrifice of convenience to revenue.

Of social reform there was very little idea. Prisons were pest-houses, scenes of every moral and physical evil that can be imagined. Debtors, who might be confined for life if they could not satisfy their creditors, were in as wretched a plight as criminals. Women as well as men were flogged. Hanging meant slow strangulation. If a man accused of any crime refused to plead, he was liable to a lingering death of torture and starvation, known as the peine forte et dure. On the other hand, the most minutely technical flaw in the indictment was enough to defeat the ends of justice, and benefit of clergy was a defence for any one who could read, unless he had been convicted before. Nobody thought of the criminal law as a reforming agency. Punishment was mere vengeance, though the fear of the gallows was not found to deter the criminal classes from coining, or sheep-stealing, or highway robbery. Indeed war, and duels, and assassination, and smallpox, and courts of justice seem to have familiarized people's minds with the idea of death until they became callous, and almost indifferent. Insanity excited so little compassion that lunatics were used like wild beasts, and Bedlam was one of the" sights of London, with the lions at the Tower. One of the many excuses for intoxication was the badness of the water. Wells were often contaminated by cesspools or graveyards, even in London, where the New River Company supplied to those who could pay for it the only safe form of Adam's ale. Ale itself was good enough, though strong, and labouring men drank little else. Tea, which came from China, was the luxury of the rich, and chocolate found much favour with women of fashion, who also took snuff as freely as their modern successors smoke cigarettes. Pipes, the only method of smoking then practised, were common in all classes of society, and for the well-to-do there was abundance of excellent wine from France, Spain, Portugal, or Italy. Bolingbroke was especially fond of "Florence wine," probably Chianti or Montepulciano. Fuel, like food, was cheap and plentiful, England being still overgrown with timber. Coal, however, which came to London by sea from Northumberland, and from Scotland, was dear on account of carriage. The mixture of damp from the river with the smoke of coal from chimneys had not begun to poison the atmosphere of the capital.

The social position of the clergy at the commencement of the eighteenth century has been the subject of much dispute. Mr. Gladstone vehemently protested, and ingeniously argued, that Macaulay had decried and underrated it as it was in the reign of William the Third. Macaulay may have been on this, as on some other occasions, too rhetorical. His own eloquence, though usually supported by profound knowledge, was apt to carry him away. But most of the available evidence shows that he was substantially right, and it was not in Anne's power, much as she would have liked, to effect a change. She was herself excessively conventional, a great stickler for the observance of rank and etiquette. She considered Matthew Prior socially unfit to represent her at Paris. When Bolingbroke approached her in a "Ramillies," or bob wig, instead of the full-bottomed peruke, she said, "I suppose his lordship will soon be coming to Court in his night-cap." It is true that the high places in the Church of England, with all the precedence they involve, have always been open to men of plebeian origin, though they have often been bestowed upon otherwise unqualified cadets of ennobled houses. But between bishops and inferior clergy the distance in the eighteenth century was immeasurable. Before Anne came to the throne Tillotson, a man of real eminence, had been succeeded as Archbishop of Canterbury by Tenison, formerly Bishop of Lincoln, a Low Churchman and a Whig, too warm a friend of the Hanoverian Succession to please the Queen. She preferred Archbishop Sharp of York, whom she appointed a Commissioner for the Scottish Union, and Bishop Compton of London, who had confirmed her. Compton was an active politician, an ardent Protestant, and a very able man. His colleagues were not distinguished, with the exception of Burnet, Bishop of Salisbury, the historian, Sprat, Bishop of Rochester, joint author of the Rehearsal, and Atterbury, a Jacobite politician rather than a High Church divine, who succeeded Sprat in 1713. The country clergymen of this date were, as a rule, miserably poor, unless they were pluralists. The landed class, the squires, did not recognize them as equals. When Sir Roger de Coverley went to church, it was for him, not for the parson, that the congregation rose. Yorick in Tristram Shandy is a scholar, a gentleman, and a humorist. But then Yorick is Sterne himself, put back into an older time. Tusher in Esmond is a more faithful copy. What Thackeray says is not evidence for the historian of Queen Anne. It is when we go to Thackeray's sources, to Addison and Swift, or even to Fielding, who was near enough in date for all practical purposes, that we find out the fidelity of the portraits in that literary masterpiece. Fielding's Parson Trulliber is, no doubt, a rather gross caricature. His Parson Adams, on the other hand, is a type of the best, not the worst, and shows therefore conclusively how low the clerical profession then ranked in the esteem of the vulgar, "both the great vulgar and the small." The domestic chaplain, the "tame Levite," was a feature of social life in those days, and such posts in wealthy establishments were earnestly coveted. "For my own part," says Addison, whose respect for the Church marked him out from his literary friends, "I have often blushed to see a gentleman, whom I know to have much more wit and learning than myself, and who was bred up with me at the University upon the same footing of a Liberal Education, treated in such an ignominious manner, and sunk beneath those of his own rank, by reason of that Character, which ought to bring him honour." It is difficult to account for this sentiment at a time when the political influence of the Church was almost unbounded. A partial explanation may perhaps be found in the current idea of a gentleman as a man who fought duels, which a clergyman obviously could not do. Addison knew what he was writing about, and it seems useless to support him by a host of minor authorities. One great name will suffice. Swift, when he was in London, lived with statesmen, authors, and fine ladies, not with clergymen. But he felt and resented every slight to his cloth. When he was at Windsor in 1711, and the object of emulous attentions from the society of the Court, he wrote to Stella, "I never dined with the chaplains till to-day; but my friend Gastrell, and the Dean of Rochester (Pratt) had often invited me, and I happened to be disengaged: it is the worst provided table at Court. We ate on pewter: every chaplain, when he is made a dean, gives a piece of plate, and so they have got a little, some of it very old. One who was made Dean of Peterborough (a small deanery) said he would give no plate; he was only Dean of Pewterborough." Swift elsewhere contrasts the triumph of aspiring mediocrity with the neglect of modest genius. Such comparisons have been made, and such morals have been drawn, in other callings and at other times. If Swift, who was doubtless thinking of himself, had gone to the Bar, his advancement would probably have been more rapid, and would certainly have been less exposed to criticism. There was not much spiritual fervour in the Church of Anne, and the drinking habits of the period were not confined to the laity. The level of the sermon, always written, was not high, and the best sermons of the day have been not ill described as essays from the Spectator without the Addisonian elegance. Religious life was more active among the Dissenters, who had the stimulus of persecution. Edmund Calamy, a Presbyterian, and Matthew Henry, who was a lawyer before he became a Nonconformist minister, enjoyed a just reputation as devout and learned theologians. Daniel Burgess, whose chapel was destroyed by the mob at the time of Sacheverell's impeachment, had something of Hugh Latimer's popular eloquence and racy wit. Buried in the ponderous tomes, which contain the verse and prose of Isaac Watts, is a quaint example of the hopes and the disappointment inspired by the accession of Anne, and by her surrender to Toryism. In the year which followed the battle of Blenheim, Watts addressed to the Queen a congratulatory Ode, in which, with reference to the Old Pretender, then young, her Majesty is loyally assured that —

"The vengeance of thy rod, with general joy

Shall scourge rebellion and the rival boy."

Sixteen years later, in 1721, Watts republished this Ode, appending to it, however, a Palinode or recantation. "George, not Anne," he explained, "was the name of promise. The latter part of Anne's reign was by no means attended with the accomplishment of those glorious hopes which we had conceived."

"'Twas George diffused a vital ray,

And gave the dying nations day:

His influence soothes the Russian bear,

Calms rising wars, and heals the air."

The doctor is still sanguine, and cheerfulness is its own reward. Very slowly, and at very long intervals, did the Nonconformists obtain freedom and justice from hostile Tories and lukewarm Whigs. For the free churches the last four years of Queen Anne were the darkest hour before the dawn.

At William's death, even more than at James's flight, the fate of England trembled in the balance. His profound designs for securing the cause of Protestantism were cut short by the "little gentleman in black," and Anne was quite incapable of understanding them, or carrying them on. No one foresaw, no one could foresee, that at that precise moment an English soldier as sagacious in counsel as supreme in war would step to the front, and lead Europe against Louis. Still less could it have been predicted that the general would be able to control the sovereign, not by his own splendid talents and subtle manoeuvres, but by the personal ascendency of his wife over the Queen. The Duchess of Marlborough's personal government did not last for ever, but it lasted just long enough. When it began, France was supreme. When it ended, France was insignificant. The reign of Anne is the reign of Marlborough, who might have restored under conditions either James the Second or the Old Pretender. Whatever may be the theological depth or value of his Protestantism, it saved England, and preserved the liberties of Europe. The Toryism of the last four years, though not ostensibly Jacobite, alarmed the mercantile community, and thus fostered the growth of the Hanoverian Whigs. If Oxford and Bolingbroke had acted more like Solomon, less like Rehoboam, they might have retained, or at least shared, supreme power even after the death of the Queen. They did what the Whigs would have wished them to do, and played into the hands of their political adversaries. Walpole and the Hanoverian Succession were the natural consequences that ensued.

To sum up: the reign of Anne was distinguished by splendid military achievements, by great material prosperity, by supreme excellence in literature, and by the auspicious union of England with Scotland. Of scientific discovery there was little, and of social reform there was less. Triennial Parliaments, and a disputed succession, were injurious to political stability. An Erastian Church reared its mitred head against heresy rather than against vice, and thought more of excluding Dissenters from power than of promoting Christianity among the people. Tories upheld the establishment, and Whigs became champions of Nonconformity, for their own factious and selfish ends. While politicians struggled for place, the mass of the people were forgotten. Those Englishmen who adhered to the ancient faith, and acknowledged the authority of Rome, were shut out from public life, and could only further the interests of their religion by rebellion or by intrigue. The bulk of the nation, absorbed in making money and enjoying life, were ready to accept any form of Government which gave them tranquillity and order. England was self-supporting, thinly peopled, imperfectly cultivated, yielding an ample profit to the makers of English cloth, the diggers of English coal, and the tillers of English soil. Except wine and tobacco, the former a luxury of the rich, scarcely anything in general use came from abroad, for tea, coffee, and chocolate had a limited vogue. The England of Anne was scarcely more conscious than the England of Elizabeth that this island would become the centre of an Empire bounded only by the limits of the world. Elizabethan seamanship, with all its dazzling intrepidity, is a record of personal adventure, and the navy of Queen Anne, despite the almost accidental capture of Gibraltar, did little to be compared with the achievements of her army. Although the freedom and independence of England were directly threatened by the pretensions of Louis, Englishmen did not readily understand why they should go on fighting for the balance of power. The oldest of those British colonies which still retain their allegiance dates from the Treaty of Utrecht. But little was thought of Newfoundland at the time, and Bolingbroke very naturally laid more stress upon the retention of Gibraltar, as a sign of British ascendency in the politics of Europe. The American colonies notwithstanding. Queen Anne's Ministers did not look beyond the sphere of European diplomacy. Even Ireland was to them a foreign, conquered nation, and the Highlands of Scotland little better than a den of thieves. If the Jacobites looked to France, the eyes of Whigs, and of Hanoverian Tories, were bent upon the Empire and upon Holland. Charles the Second and his brother had not succeeded in destroying the monarchical sentiment, the spirit of personal loyalty, in the minds of Englishmen who believed that the Revolution of 1688 was the smaller of two evils. How much the story of the warming-pan, and the general credit which it received, had to do with the Act of Settlement and the Hanoverian dynasty, we cannot tell. George the First was accepted as a King in fact by many who regarded James Stuart as King in law. Even now, when nobody argues in favour of divine right, the direct descent of the Sovereign from James the First is a circumstance of immense practical value. George was not a mere stranger like William. Anne was not a stranger at all. The Jacobites could urge nothing but her sex against her claim, and her sex appealed to the chivalry of her subjects. Marlborough would never have prostrated himself before a man as he did before her. William the Third had to depend entirely upon his own courage, clemency, and statecraft. Anne was a Stuart, and her person was sacred. She showed sympathy with her people by attending Parliament, subscribing to the Church, touching for the King's Evil. She set an example of conjugal fidelity and private decorum. She was generous without being extravagant, and virtuous without being Puritanical. She owned racehorses, and her husband was a regular attendant at Newmarket. Her prejudice against Dissenters was not unpopular, and she gave no countenance to the licentiousness of the stage. Her indifference to literature did her no harm with the middle classes, whose representative she really was. When they were for war, she was for w-ar. When she was for peace, they were for peace. In the reign of Elizabeth the people worshipped their magnificent Queen. When the imperial votaress passed on, in maiden meditation fancy free, they bowed their heads. She was the equal in scholarship and in statecraft of the ablest Ministers round her throne. She was too much above ordinary folk for the common sort of popularity. Anne's mind was like thousands of other minds. She felt and thought with her people. Even her confusions were theirs. They were not in theory averse from passive obedience, so long as it was not translated into practice. They approved of Whiggery, so far as it had delivered them from Popery and wooden shoes. They suspected Whigs of being half Republicans, and Republicanism had no support. If Protestantism meant hatred of Popery, they were Protestants, and so was the Queen. If it meant Puritanism, and the Conventicle, she detested it, and so did they. The freethinking Electress Sophia would have shocked public opinion, and Anne at least kept Sophia from the throne. Between 1702 and 1714 the English nation had time to consider the future, and to make up their minds. Their Sovereign was thoroughly English, though her Scottish origin was not forgotten north of the Tweed. She did not intrigue with foreign powers, and her people never had to pay her debts. Her domestic sorrows, especially the little Duke of Gloucester's death, appealed to the hearts of her future subjects before her reign began. In her subsequent quarrel with the Duchess of Marlborough she had the sympathetic support of all who disliked tyranny and ingratitude. When she refused to make the Duke Captain General for life, her conduct appealed to the national hatred of a military dictatorship. When she dismissed Godolphin and the Whigs, she was at least rebelling against tutelage, and behaving like a Queen. Her dignified answer to the rude request of Parliament that she should marry again touched the heart of every wife and mother who respected herself. The pettiness of court life, which abounded in the Court of Anne, was unknown to the public. They knew, and liked to know, that the Queen disapproved of Bolingbroke, and would not make Swift a bishop. Even her unreasoning patronage of Sacheverell, brawler and mischief-maker as he was, could be made to look like hatred of persecution; and for the Schism Act, which certainly was persecution, her Majesty's Ministers, together with Parliament itself, were responsible. Her obstinate refusal to see the Electress, or the Elector, or the Electoral Prince, her statutory heirs, was just one of those human weaknesses which common folk appreciate and understand. Anne has not found many enthusiastic admirers besides Miss Strickland. But she has a useful, and even an honourable, place in history: she bridged a gulf, and supplied a want. Her reign of splendour abroad, and peace at home, smoothed the path of constitutional progress through that loyal passion for our temperate kings which our great poet has described.

A NOTE TO THE READER

WE HOPED YOU LOVED THIS BOOK. IF YOU DID, PLEASE LEAVE A REVIEW ON AMAZON TO LET EVERYONE ELSE KNOW WHAT YOU THOUGHT.

WE WOULD ALSO LIKE TO THANK OUR SPONSORS **WWW.DIGITALHISTORYBOOKS.COM** WHO MADE THE PUBLICATION OF THIS BOOK POSSIBLE.

WWW.DIGITALHISTORYBOOKS.COM PROVIDES A WEEKLY NEWSLETTER OF THE BEST DEALS IN HISTORY AND HISTORICAL FICTION.

SIGN UP TO THEIR NEWLSETTER TO FIND OUT MORE ABOUT THEIR LATEST DEALS.

Printed by Amazon Italia Logistica S.r.l.
Torrazza Piemonte (TO), Italy

11877156R00093